MW01532371

DOUG

ENJOY LIFE'S

MOMENTS!

LIFE
IN MOMENTS

Inspiration, Determination, Grit

www.LifeInMoments.com

Inky
Press

Life In Moments

Copyright © 2021 by Tom Hart

All rights reserved.

Permission to reproduce or transmit in any form or by any means, electronic or mechanical, including photocopying, photographic and recording audio or video, or by any information storage and retrieval system, must be obtained in writing from the author.

Life In Moments, written by Tom Hart.

To order additional copies of this title, e-mail:
tom@lifeinmoments.com

Information about this book and the author may be found here:

website: lifeinmoments.com

First printing September 2021

Library of Congress Cataloging-in-Publication Data

      Hart, Tom
      Life in moments : inspiration, determination, grit / by Tom Hart
        p. cm
        ISBN: 9798467144856
        1. Leadership. 2. Self help. 3. Personal growth.
        4. Happiness. 5. Self esteem. 6. Management.
        7. Personal success.

Published by Inky Press a division of Incubate Media, LLC.

Printed in the U.S.A.

14 13 12 11 10   1 2 3 4 5 6 7 8 9 10

Dedicated to my grandchildren
Emma and Damien.

I will forever cherish our moments together.

Acknowledgements

I feel a deep sense of gratitude to the following people for making this book come to life.

To my writing coach and friend Roger Brooks whom I have known for over 10 years...
I learned so much from you during this journey. You have such a kind, and thought-provoking way of bringing out the best in people. I discovered something new in each of our Saturday weekly meetings. I honestly feel I would not have finished this book without your help and inspiration.

To my daughter Gillian Zamora...
Thank you so much for the editing, gentle nudging to say more and inspiring me to do better. I'm so fortunate to have such a bright and talented daughter help me write my first book – what a moment to cherish!

Table of Contents

Introduction

"Life is not measured by time. It is measured by moments."

—Armin Houman

A parent takes you for a ride one sunny afternoon. A co-worker lingers a minute before leaving the room. A partner says a few encouraging words before you begin another day. A young man meets your gaze as he hands you back your change at the local corner store. A young child gets a reassuring smile that says we are going to be ok.

These might seem like ordinary moments, unremarkable really.

But what if they were life changing, and you didn't even know it? What if they happened at a time when that person needed reassurance, a warm smile, or a tender moment.

These encounters with the people in your life are stitched together and become the fabric of your past. But more than our past, these moments etched in your memory can lift you from your darkest moments.

In Life In Moments, I explore the seismic impact the smallest of gestures can provide. What you may have thought was a simple encounter, a few words of encouragement, a gentle nod of support, may be the lifeblood of someone's sheer will to go forward and meet the challenges life has to offer.

Join me in this journey to explore how these encounters impacted my life at the right moment, and more importantly how these moments carried me through some of the most difficult days in my life. A quick glance at my resume seeing a career spanning a stock clerk rising to chief operating officer and launching my own business would seem to conjure up word associations of hard-work, determination, grit. Some of that is true, but that is not the story. I didn't want to write another business book extolling a philosophy of success.

Instead, I wanted to share my most vulnerable moments along the way. The failures, fears and roadblocks that never make it to short bios and introductions. How those same fears, failures and roadblocks were really gifts that I would treasure for a lifetime.

A resume also leaves off the people who inspired you and provided the push you needed when you wanted to step back.

When you finish this book, I hope for two things:

1. Each day you have an opportunity to impact someone's life with even the smallest gestures.

2. If you are feeling fearful, have doubts, or setbacks, you realize that you are not alone. Everyone has those same experiences. It's how you use them to gain experience and inspire you in the future.

Our moments, seemingly small unremarkable moments, are really quite remarkable.

Life in Moments. A journey to share together.

Chapter 1

Recognizing Your Grit Moment
A Simple Task, A Defining Moment

"Use what talents you possess; the woods will be very silent if no birds sang there except those that sang best."

—Henry van Dyke

I grew up in a town that had grit, but my personal grit didn't really make an appearance until the late '70s. My journey to understanding the power of grit and determination began in 1978 in Buffalo, New York when I was 18 years old. The Western New York city, also known as the City of Good Neighbors, prided itself on its gritty reputation and blue-collar jobs. It was a decent-sized city with a small-town feel to it. Buffalo was once booming with steel and automotive factories that provided good-paying jobs. But over time many of those buildings became boarded-up relics of yesteryear. My hometown is also known for its love of football (Go Bills!), months of endless snow, relishing its underdog roots, and food creations such as beef on weck and, of course, hot chicken wings.

I grew up in a family of six in South Buffalo where you identified with the parish you belonged to – mine was Saint Martins. I was the youngest in the family with two sisters and a brother. My father worked in one of the factories and my mother was a waitress. It was a pretty standard family existence for my neighborhood at the time. My parents, along with my friends' parents, were raised during the depression. So we'd often hear those stories of "When I was a kid, we didn't have TV and we played outside all day" or something similar. As a young teen at the time, I would roll my eyes as if to say, "Whatever." In my later years, I learn more about the experiences my parents endured during the '20s and '30s and listen intensely as my father described how the deliveryman would bring a giant block of ice to sit in their refrigerator, or back then an "icebox." I finally figured out why he would say, "Tommy, put the milk back in the icebox." It literally was an icebox.

I was a senior in high school and those days were not the brightest memories for me. I couldn't wait to get out. At school, I was the type of kid you might not remember. You certainly wouldn't associate the memory of me with grit. I was an introvert to the extreme, avoided parties, searched for the quietest lunch tables and stayed close to only a few friends who didn't push me to be someone I wasn't. My mother would always say, "Tommy, what's the matter? Smile more." Her words made me feel even more self-conscious. What was wrong with me?

Any chance of being in the spotlight meant a potential panic attack. And high school had a way of putting you in the spotlight, like in gym class. For some reason, several times a year, we had to play baseball during gym class in the school parking lot. I remember being stuck in the outfield thinking, *Please God, don't let them hit the ball to me.* I knew I had zero chance of catching that ball. I can still remember the day the ball was headed straight for me though — it was like slow motion as I raised my mitt in the air, more to shield my face from getting pummeled from a baseball dropping from the sky rather than setting up to catch it. But for a split second I thought, *I think I can catch this.* Then I heard the sound of the ball slap the pavement, about 6 feet from me. How could I have been that far off? Someone else grabbed the ball and tossed it to another player. It was one of those moments you hope quickly fades from peoples' memories and no one remembers. I remember at the time thinking if I don't have eye contact with anyone it will be like it never happened. I obviously didn't forget.

I was struggling to find my way, and depressed about my future. My brother and sisters were getting married, having kids, and buying homes. It seemed like everyone had their entire existence planned. Me? I had no idea what I wanted to do. My mother wanted me to work at the post office, and my dream from a young age of being a linebacker for the Buffalo Bills wasn't possible because of the whole "I'm horrible at sports" thing.

All that changed one day. I was walking along Potters Road that winter in 1978 with these thoughts swirling around in my head when I noticed out of the corner of my eye an abandoned building now had a sign stating, "Wilson Farms – Opening Soon - Help Wanted." I was working in the housekeeping department at Mercy Hospital at the time but was curious about this opportunity. It would be walking distance from my house if I got a job there. I'm not sure what drew me to take notice and consider applying, but I was intrigued nonetheless. I was familiar with Wilson Farms as the local convenience store – everyone was really. Back then, most convenience stores didn't have gas since that was sold at automotive repair shops. But they typically had a deli, snacks, beer, soft drinks, and pantry items like milk, bread, and eggs to get your family through the week.

I decided to go with my gut and apply for the job. They hired me. *A new beginning!* I thought. I now hold the title of stock clerk! I remember the night before the store opened like it was yesterday. The president of the company, Dick Moscati, came to tell us how proud he was of the new store opening and to thank us for being part of the team. It was the dead of winter, and the melting snow was slipping off his boots as he spoke, making a small puddle where he stood. *I'll clean that up after he leaves*, I thought. Something about his tone and genuineness gave me a really warm feeling on this winter day and a sudden sense of belonging. I was part of a team that didn't leave me standing in the outfield in panic mode. We were in it together. Dick was an impressive man. He was as genuine as they come with an enthusiasm I hadn't experienced before. I could tell he loved his job and had a passion for what he was doing. I'm convinced that his enthusiasm and genuine excitement became attached to me somehow that day and lasted a lifetime. It was exactly what I needed at that moment.

The next person I would meet was John Brockenshire, the store manager. Little did I know at the time that John would change my life and be responsible for unlocking my grit. He would become the inspiration I was searching for.

John was probably in his early 40s, and everything you would expect in a Buffalonian. He always had a big smile on his face, red cheeks, and talked a bit out of the side of his mouth. "Thomas, my friend, it's good to see you!" was a greeting I would hear often over the coming years. He was always rushing around, taking care of business. I remember how he had this unique ability to watch everything that was going on around him while continuing to work and greet almost every person who walked in the door with that crooked, genuine smile. I admired him from the moment we met. I wasn't really sure why, but he was different from the other adults at school, my friends' parents, and the workers at Mercy Hospital, where I had been working. I didn't know at the time, but John would become my first mentor. When I met him, I felt something unique, as if I crossed a threshold in time, and started anew.

In John's store we were always on the go, moving from task to task. From the moment I punched the clock until I left, I felt like I belonged. It was indescribable really. I suddenly had purpose and John gave me the confidence I was sorely lacking. He kept giving me more and more responsibility, reassurances, and, always, a smile. John took the time to remind this 18-year-old kid that he had value, and a place where he was welcome.

This is the job, as a stock clerk, in which I faced grit for the first time. Perhaps it seems like a quite unremarkable job. Most people might shrug their shoulders and say, "What's the big deal?" Well, I'll tell you the deal.

On this particular day, John called and asked me to come in early. This happened quite often when someone called in sick, or he just needed some help. My shift was typically 4 p.m. to midnight. He knew I'd always say yes, and it was a 15-minute walk from my house. I was typically out the door and ready for work in minutes. Truth be told, I had hoped to be called in early most days, or even on my day off. It wasn't for the additional $2.65 an hour I would get, it was about spending more time in a place I came to love.

We received several deliveries that day and things seemed a bit more hectic than usual. John was putting on his jacket as he was letting me know what needed to be done that night. "Can you fill the cooler and get things organized? I have to leave early," he said as he rushed down the aisle, walking sideways so he could give instructions to me and get out the front door as quickly as possible. "Sure thing, sounds good," I said, which was my typical reply to all requests from John.

As he headed out, I opened the heavy cooler door latch to peer inside. What was before my eyes was not what I expected. Boxes filled with soda, beer, milk, and produce were everywhere from one end to the other, piled high to the ceiling, and the shelves to the cooler were half empty. Some of the stacks toppled over, and I could see broken glass. The smell of stale beer filled the air.

John trusted *me* to get this job done? This seemed like a job that would take days, not hours. *I have other things to do besides spending the entire night in here*, I thought.

During my night shift, I was responsible for stocking the store, giving the cashiers a break from the register, helping in the deli, making a deposit, and anything else that happened during the night shift. I was buzzed in to go up front to help for a few moments, which broke me from my trance of surveying the disaster in the cooler. As I later headed back to the cooler to handle the situation, I felt an overwhelming sense of determination. *I got this*. This isn't the outfield and I'm not going to fail. Besides, John trusted me to get this done and I'm not about to disappoint him now.

I poured myself into the task at hand with an energy and conviction that soared. I was filled with an emotion I didn't understand, or even experience before today. By the time I was done, the cooler shelves were full, the backstock was organized neatly, and the floors were clear. In fact, I came up with an entirely new system for how everything was set and labeled. I didn't want to stop. I bleached the floor and continued using my newfound source of energy to organize the rest of the store. I found myself multitasking just like John. A fire was lit. By the end of the night, I was cleaning up the backroom, where people hung their jackets, and the bottle return area, and just about anywhere that looked out of place. I felt like, for the first time, my efforts had real meaning.

As I walked home just after midnight and looked up at the cold night sky, everything seemed more aligned up there. Something inside me changed and it felt great. I was introduced to grit and determination that night and I liked the way we got along. We were destined to be good friends in the years ahead. I would come calling them many more times to see me through the challenges in my work and life.

When I arrived at work the next day, John said the usual, "Thomas my friend, it's good to see you!" But he had an extra big grin today and was shooting me a mysterious look, squinting his eyes a bit. "What got into you last night?" *Wait, did I not do a great job? I thought I did.* "What do you mean?" I asked a bit sheepishly. "I mean you bleached the entire backroom and cooler last night?" For a second I thought, *Was I not supposed to do that?* "Yes, is that ok?" I replied. "OK?," John exclaimed. "The store looked cleaner than when we opened it. In fact, the entire store looked incredible!" I summoned a reply back, something like, "Thanks, John." As I turned away, I felt a smile on my face growing and a deep sense of satisfaction I never felt before.

John would eventually give me more and more responsibility. A few months later, I was closing the store at night and making deposits at the bank on the way home after closing. Me, Tommy Hart, an official store-closer at Wilson Farms, with keys to the castle — or the front door at least. Yes, my siblings were still surpassing me, and everyone wanted me to get a more "stable" job like my brother and sisters had. But this felt right to me.

John mentored me to become an assistant manager and eventually a store manager. We became good friends and kept in touch for many years. We would often meet at Red Lalley's corner tavern, or "gin mill" as my father often called a local bar for some reason. It was a neighborhood bar owned by Red where everyone knew each other. It had a unique aroma of hot sauce, fried foods, and draft beer all mixed together that was identifiable to most establishments in Buffalo. I always felt like the youngest patron in the bar as the row of stools across from me was full of retired men, drinking tall glasses of beer with a whiskey chaser, spinning tales about the old neighborhood and when they were young. John and I would enjoy a few draft beers together and talk about life. I'd share some frustrations, seeking his sage advice, and he always delivered.

The years went by, and we drifted apart as often happens over time. I never got to say goodbye to John, thank him, and tell him how much he meant to me. When I went back to Buffalo for my father's funeral, I drove by Red's tavern and a flood of warm memories filled my heart. I remember turning the car around and sitting in the parking lot for a few minutes and thinking about how lucky I was to have John in my life. Life has a way of letting friendships slip away, only to be cherished in later years. I never shared the impact his one night of confidence had on a kid that saw his life going nowhere and was deeply lost and depressed. I waited too long. But thinking back on our time spent at Red Lalley's sharing a story, a laugh and a true friendship - I think deep down he knew I needed a mentor.

My Moment of Reflection

I didn't know it at the time, but that one night, that one moment, opened the door to me having the confidence to understand what it takes to succeed. This feeling of diving in and pushing through the challenges in life could now be summoned at any time. The key for me was recognizing that I could accomplish something I'd never faced before. It helped drive me from stock clerk to becoming chief operating officer in the convenience store industry.

Understanding how I got there is key to unlocking this energy and achieving success throughout my life. On the night I found my grit, it really was an unremarkable accomplishment in the scheme of great moments in one's life. It happens everyday without making headline news. But for an 18-year-old kid, depressed and having no sense of belonging, it's exactly what I needed. I felt hungry for this feeling in the years ahead. I never forgot and had the opportunity to witness over and over again people who had that same sense of pride and accomplishment early in their careers. I tried to provide encouragement in even the simplest of encounters. It could be their moment. I wanted it to be special and memorable.

But what triggered me? I think it was wanting to prove to myself, not to others, that I could find my path in life and blaze my own trail. Yes, my mother still wanted me to get a job at the post office and many of my friends and family were getting married, finishing college, and buying homes. But I was enjoying where I was in life for the first time, probably ever. And I never wanted to lose that feeling. I hadn't figured out how to summon grit outside of work yet. But inside those four walls of a convenience store, I felt like I could accomplish anything.

We all have proud moments in our life. They may make us laugh, or shed a tear. Some moments we wish we could relive again. Understanding your moment that changed your direction or gave you confidence, what triggered you, and using it as fuel throughout your life, can help carry you through the most difficult of times.

These moments of newfound confidence may seem rather small and insignificant at first. But it all starts somewhere, and you keep building on each moment, day to day, month to month, year to year.

I'll share with you the moments that carried me from that stock clerk in Buffalo New York, to Chief Operating Officer of a convenience store chain in Boston and eventually managing my own technology business. It was filled with its share of challenges, but my experiences with the people around me carried me to places I never thought I would experience. Let's go!

Chapter 2

Two Paths, One Direction

"You will recognize your own path when you come upon it, because you will suddenly have all the energy and imagination you will ever need."

—Jerry Gillies

During that same summer of 1978, I got a taste of the factory life that Buffalo was known for.

Each summer, a certain number of employees' relatives would get the opportunity to work for eight weeks to earn good factory pay and gain some experience. My father was a supervisor at Trico Plant No. 1 at the time, managing the first floor. Temporary summer help was available, so I gave it a shot while keeping my nighttime job working as a stock clerk/closer in a convenience store.

Trico's design was called a "daylight factory," featuring floor-to-ceiling windows letting in light and a breath of outside air. Not that you ever really smelled a fresh summer breeze, but at least it felt less closed-in. The plant was constructed in the 1920s with Trico becoming the first manufacturer of windshield wipers. The story behind Trico's founder, John Oishei, was that he was driving down Delaware Avenue in Buffalo and collided with a bicyclist during a rainstorm. This experience caused Oishei to become interested in creating a way to maintain vision on a rainy night. The cyclist was not seriously injured, but it was enough to inspire him to act. [*1]. From there, Trico grew, especially after World War II, as a major employer in the area.

I would travel to work with my father at his usual time of 5:30 a.m., but my work didn't begin until 7 a.m. His work didn't begin until then either, but he would get in early, read the local paper, the *Buffalo Courier-Express*, and have his coffee and breakfast, buttered toast, while the plant was silent. There was almost an eerie quiet at that time of the day. I guess he liked to center himself before the factory awoke and workers flooded the factory floors, fired up the machines and forklifts.

I sat at a table across from his desk, waiting for my shift to start. We never really talked much. I guess I wanted to respect his morning routine. I remember one morning in particular, in the quietness of his office, I thought how lucky I was to have a dad as special as mine.

I didn't know it at the time, but my father was my lifelong mentor. A World War II veteran whose focus in life was taking care of his family. His education went as far as the 8th grade in the 1930s, but here he was supervising the entire floor of Trico Plant #1. My father was a quiet man who didn't talk about himself much - ever.

When I was growing up, he kept busy around the house with projects, big and small. I remember him building a deck for our pool by himself in a single weekend. He could replace a window, fix the furnace, and remodel the basement on his own as well. There were no YouTube videos back then so I'm sure it was a talent he always had, most likely because of growing up in the depression and relying on logic and bare hands as his greatest tool. He was always tinkering with our cars too; Oil changes, spark plugs, starters, and trips to the junkyard to find a replacement part. He didn't have a passion for cars, he simply needed to keep them running.

He would always know when something was bothering me, or I was just sad for no real reason.

I remember one day I was feeling particularly down. I can't remember exactly why. He noticed me brooding and said, "C'mon, we're going for a ride." I think I was around 10 years old. I said "Ok", not really knowing where we were going. I assumed we were going to the store or to visit a relative. I asked somewhere along the ride, "Where are we going?" He just responded with, "We are almost there." To my surprise and delight, we arrived at the Erie County Fair!

The fair was a big event in Buffalo with rides, games, shows, and all the typical food you would expect: Candy apples, cotton candy, sausages. The smell of fried dough filled the summer air as we pulled into the grass parking lot.

We got out of the car. "Let's go play some games," he said. We used to call it carnival row, because you could play anything from tossing darts to knocking over milk cans with a baseball. "Step right up! Win a prize!" I was never any good at knocking things down, but that didn't matter here. I had the best time going from game to game. I remember he kept letting me play and I thought *Wow, we must be rich,* because each game cost money to play.

We came upon this rope ladder that really looked like a hammock. You had to climb up and ring the bell without tipping over. I was nervous about trying it with people watching, but Dad encouraged me to give it a try. I was shaking, the ladder was shaking. But I made it to the top and rang the bell! As I looked back, I could see my father steadying the rope ladder with one hand, helping me out, while sharing a smile with the ride operator. I wasn't disappointed that I hadn't achieved the win on my own. I remember feeling so happy that my dad was there to support me. I always knew from that moment on, I could count on him for love, support, and always being there for me.

I had this warm feeling once again as I watched him turn the page of his morning newspaper.

At 7 a.m. sharp, after everyone punched the clock, the factory awoke with a loud clamor. I had two types of roles at Trico that summer. The first was putting rivets in two parts of wiper blades to connect them together. Seemed easy enough. I sat at this giant table that had a smell resembling the oil I would put on my bike chain. The job: Place one part on the left, connecting the part on the right. You place the two together, one over the other, and press down on the floor pedal to insert the rivet. The pile was enormous. I thought it would take the whole day to handle just one pile, but learned it would be filled over and over again all day long.

I remember a wall clock positioned just over my shoulder to the left, the windows next to it tilted open to give us a glimpse of the outside and providing a ray of sunshine to sneak through. It was as if the sun and the city itself would be tucked away until we were done with our work, but leave us a tiny reminder they'd be waiting for us. I had been dutifully putting my wiper parts together for what seems like an eternity. I peered up at the clock I spotted earlier and noted the time – 7:20 a.m.? It has only been 20 minutes? How will I make it to 3:00 p.m.?

My next role at Trico was a trucker. Not the kind that drives an 18-wheeler, but someone with a two-wheeler, a metal hook, and a willingness to run all over the plant floor. A trucker replenished the parts for the people at the tables assembling the parts. They would hand you a card, you'd get the parts, bring them to the worker, and dump them on the table. Sounds easy right? It was the perfect job for someone who had a basic understanding of factory parts. That was not me.

They would yell out "trucker" and I would run

over, get their card, and off I'd go. If I was late, I could cost them money since they had a financial incentive to assemble a higher number than the time-study noted they could handle. Needless to say, I fell behind almost immediately. It wasn't for a lack of hustling. I was eating up time trying to determine what part matched this card they handed me. There was a sea of parts that seemed to stretch to eternity and to me they all looked similar. All I could hear was the shouts of "trucker" and I realized this job was not for me.

I had, and have today, a deep respect for people who work in that factory. It was hard, focused work in an environment that didn't allow much interaction with each other until breaktime or lunch. The whistle would blow, and everyone stopped. During these times I can remember a camaraderie amongst the workers that seemed quite special. Sometimes they would catch up on family news, argue about football, or chat about current events of any kind. Coffee and cigarettes were the mainstay at breaktime, and the typical lunch was what you would expect in a metal lunch box in 1978. At that time, most were feasting on a white-bread sandwich, with a thermos of some sort of beverage. From what I gathered, some of those beverages were spiked with a splash of whiskey, but I minded my own business. I was the summer help, a short timer, who was positioned at the end of the table, respecting the regulars.

I didn't bring an official lunch box; the recognizable brown paper bag was my carrier of choice. Getting something nicer seemed like an investment not worthy for summer help. I would always walk over to the row of machines and get a can of pop. As I sat at the lunch table eating my Wonder bread bologna sandwich, listening to the chatter, my mind drifted to both of my workplaces.

I enjoyed working inside of a convenience store. Something about the freedom of arriving for work and moving from task to task, being on the sales floor, the small team collaboration, and customers coming and going was liberating. Yes, there were certain things that needed to be done, but I was allowed to think for myself on how to best accomplish those responsibilities.

This seemed to be where I was most happy and increased my level of confidence. Inside those four walls of the store, I could succeed through hard work, something I came to realize was very appealing to me. It's not that the factory work was easy - it wasn't. But for me, the harder I worked at the factory, I didn't get that same feeling of accomplishment.

I put the factory life behind me and continued working in various stores over the next seven years. It was 1985 and I was 25 years old. I worked my way up from assistant manager and now had a few years as a store manager under my belt. My mother was always holding out hope that I would grow tired of the "convenience store job" and get serious about working at the post office or the local factory. "You got to have a pension!" she'd say from time to time, slapping the kitchen table for emphasis. Not really in anger, but to give the exclamation point a sound effect. She was what you might call "animated" in her speaking manner.

In her defense I think she was always worried about me – as moms often do. If there was an accident at an intersection in the neighborhood, she immediately deemed it off limits "Don't go to that intersection anymore," she'd say. "It's too dangerous." So, when I was involved in an armed robbery early on working as the stock clerk, she always had that in the back of her mind.

It happened early on when I was 18 years old, just a few months on the job, and running the register one weeknight. I was giving the associate her break. A man with a ski mask pulled down over his face walked in and pointed a gun at me and waved it at the few customers shopping at the time. I remember thinking this was a prank at first, but an accomplice pushed open the counter gate and put the barrel of his gun to the side of my head. I looked sideways at this guy. He was so close, I could feel his breath on my cheek. I knew at that point I was being held up.

I remember there was a young boy with his mother I was serving on the other side of the counter. I looked at him, then his mother, as if to say, *We're in this together, don't worry*. The man in the ski mask asked me to open the drawers.

Of course, I did. Back in 1978, we had very rudimentary alarm devices. Our registers were equipped with a silent alarm in the register till with two one-dollar bills on a clip covering the device—decoy bills. When the bills were removed, a small light would come on and notify the local police. As he was taking the money, I remember thinking he was going to see that after he removed the bills and realize it was an alarm and be angry at me for not warning him. It was so obvious to me, but he never skipped a beat. He quickly emptied both registers and off they went.

We had about 10 people in the store. I locked the front door and asked them to please wait for the police. As I headed toward the backroom to call the police in case the alarm didn't work, the police were already banging on the locked front door by the time I reached the end of the aisle. I quickly ran back to the front door and let them in.

It all seemed to happen so fast, but the replay in my mind seemed to be in slow motion. The police took statements and we re-opened fairly soon.

I put this incident behind me and stayed on my path. I loved my job and yes, by the way, I did go through my mother's banned intersection as well. Although I understood that her fears came from a good place in her heart - I needed to go my own way.

Working in retail is often an underestimated, or at least misunderstood profession. Here I was at 25 years old running a business with revenue well over a million dollars a year, managing labor costs, inventory, safety, profitability, employees, and anything else that came up in an operation that's open 365 days a year. But whenever I answered the question; "What do you do for work?" with "I manage a convenience store," people never seemed to know what to say next. If I replaced "I manage a convenience store" with "I manage a million dollar-a-year operation with dozens of employees and I am responsible with 24/7 on-call availability," I think they would have responded with "That's incredible." Instead, they would shrug their shoulders and say, "Oh. That's nice." I never let that bother me. I knew the true challenges of the job.

At that time, I was living the life of a single 25 year old whose work was his life. I had an apartment atop a pizza parlor (which caused me to have pizza for dinner at least five nights a week—no regrets) on Elmwood Avenue. The first time I heard the Bob Dylan song, "Up to Me," moved me. Released in late 1985 on his *Biograph* album which I listened to extensively, these four lines in particular stood out.

If I'd thought about it I never would've done it, I guess I would've let it slide
If I'd lived my life by what others were thinkin', the heart inside me would've died
I was just too stubborn to ever be governed by enforced insanity
Someone had to reach for the risin' star, I guess it was up to me

I wasn't going to let enforced insanity bog down my decision-making. Being a store manager felt right and I was going to go for it—no more doubts. It had been several years since my job at

Trico, but I never made a definitive decision out loud or to myself on what I wanted to do. It was at this moment I realized I wanted to stay on this path and never look back. I was proud of my career choice. I feel a deep connection working in a convenience store and still do to this day, even during a short visit in my neighborhood.

My Moment of Reflection

These two distinct experiences helped me consider two paths for my career—factory life or retail. I often wonder whether, if I didn't have John as my first boss, I would have felt lost in both experiences. But I did meet John. I can't say I thought of him or this situation in exactly those terms back then. In real time, I didn't identify John as a mentor or come up with the pros and cons of each path. But he was a mentor, nonetheless.

If I could write John a letter today, it would go something like this:

John,

I never had the opportunity to tell you how important you were in my life. Quite honestly, your mentorship, kindness, and the extra care you took gave me the confidence I needed at a time when I was feeling like a failure. I looked forward to every encounter we had and learned so much during that time.

I reflect on how fortunate I was to have met you when I mentor someone. If I can make an impact on someone's life like you did on mine, that would be my way of thanking you. Hopefully again and again, when given the opportunity.

So, thank you my friend, for all of the special moments in life together, for being there. It made a world of difference to me.

Your friend,

Tom

Choosing the right path in life can be full of challenges, mistakes, and setbacks. The pathways in our lives are often not related to work at all. It may be a new relationship that is flourishing, improving your health, fighting an addiction, or committing to volunteerism that may be tugging at your heart. To me the path was full of experiences that helped me along the way, even those that seemed painful, or dead ends at the time.

Imagine you are traveling across the country by car, and you think you have everything completely mapped out and every stop perfectly planned. But along the way you still need to refuel your car, stop for food, and find a place to rest. You may hit traffic, a detour due to a closed highway that wasn't flagged when you planned the route. You may even get lost and frustrated. There is a potential for a flat tire, accident, or mechanical breakdown. The hotel might not look like the photos on the website and you are disappointed. Even if all these things occurred, you probably never doubted you would get to your final destination. In fact, maybe these setbacks prepared you for your next road trip.

Next time, you'd check more closely for potential detours, read more reviews on where you will be staying, and perhaps take the car in for a check-up before you head out.

We can, at times, focus on the negative experiences. But we need to slow down and reflect on the positive outcomes as we choose our path. Fueling the car and finding food was easy and a good experience. The detour wasn't too far out of the way and the scenery was beautiful. In fact, 90 percent of the ride went as planned. The other 10 percent of setbacks didn't stop us from reaching our goal.

You may have a lot of doubters around you, or you may even be doubting yourself. That's to be expected. We don't want to dwell on the doubts, but rather try to understand what may be holding us back.

[*1]https://www.wkbw.com/news/john-oishei-an-industrialist-and-philanthropist

Chapter 3

Late-Night Lessons of a Lifetime

"Life's most precious moments are not all loud or uproarious. Silence and stillness has its own virtues."

—Kilroy J. Oldster

My path took a bit of a turn in March of 1986. I felt the need for a new beginning, and that meant leaving my hometown of Buffalo and starting over in a new city—Boston. Somerville, Massachusetts, just two miles north of Boston, actually. I had a friend that I grew up with that moved there years before. I had an open invitation to stay at his place in case I made the move. During one of my visits to Boston, I stopped by a convenience store named Store 24. There was a sign in the window screaming out to me: "Pick Up a Job Today!"

So, I did. I asked for an application, flew back later that month for an interview, and got the job! I would be starting as a store manager in New England to continue my journey. In my gold Ford Escort, I tossed my paper map on the passenger's seat, stuffed everything I owned in the trunk and backseat (at the time clothes, record albums and a cassette player), and headed east—almost to the shores of the Atlantic Ocean. I hopped on the NY Thruway 90 right by my house, which eventually intersected with the Mass Pike 90. That simple route took me 98 percent of the way to my new doorstep.

My friends Donnie and Dave welcomed me to stay with them for as long as I wanted, but they didn't have an extra bedroom at the time. There was a chance the other roommate might be moving out over the summer, so I staked my ground on the screened-in porch off the back of the house. There was just enough room to sleep and keep a few things in the corner. My first task was to weatherproof my living quarters. March in Boston can be wet, cold, and potentially snowy. So, I went to the hardware store and bought some plastic sheeting, a box cutter, and a staple gun. My friends gave me a few blankets and a cot, and suddenly I had a new place to lay my head at night. I knew it wasn't much—but it helped me feel like I was starting fresh. I relished in the grittiness of the moment, although there would certainly be some challenges to come.

I was ready to start my first day working as a manager-in-training at the Copley Square store on Boylston in downtown Boston. I mapped out the directions the day before to make sure I knew exactly where I was going. Finding directions in 1986 meant opening a paper map on the kitchen table and writing the directions on a piece of paper. I was a bit intimidated by the traffic in Boston. The city of Buffalo isn't exactly the town of Mayberry, where Andy Griffith lived, but it certainly wasn't Boston either.

I, per usual, arrived in Copley Square around an hour and a half before I was supposed to start my shift at the store. I found a parking garage across the street and thought—how convenient! As I turned the corner to the gate a sign came into view with the daily rates: $20 to park? For one day!? That would amount to $100 a week or about 25 percent of my paycheck, before taxes! I entered the ramp of the parking garage anyway and circled what seemed like forever to find a parking spot. I placed the ticket in my wallet to be paid later and had my moment of doubt. People warned me about the cost of living in a city like Boston, but I never wanted to hear it. Now, I was living it.

I made my way through the morning crowd and crossed Boylston Street to the store I would be training in. It was my first adventure into this part of the city. It was fast-paced and everyone who passed by appeared to be on a mission. The look on their faces seemed to shout, "Get outta my way, I have to get somewhere—quickly!" I was feeling like an outsider. But I also felt my new beginning. The street was filled with coffee shops, restaurants, clothing stores, pubs, and specialty shops. Some of the buildings seemed tall and mighty and others felt like they had been around since the colonial days. I felt exhilarated as I took in the morning air filled with the aroma of brewed coffee, fresh bagels, and sweet pastries along the way.

When I entered the store, I stopped to take in the entirety of the operation. It was tiny and so long and narrow that customers had to turn sideways to let someone by if they were walking in the same aisle. The store was filled with people and the line of customers waiting to checkout stretched down the store. The cashier was cranking through transactions with an impressive speed. Once the last customer was helped, I took this brief pause as my opening to say hello. "Hi, I'm Tom. I'm starting training today." I didn't exactly get the warm greeting I was expecting. No customary "Hi, nice to meet you" with an exchange of names. Instead, he gave me an expressionless look, pointed to the back of the store, and said, "Manager's upstairs." I'm not sure any less effort could have been given except for completely ignoring me.

I shrugged it off and made my way down the

aisle to the back of the store and up the stairs. As I reached the last step, I turned to my left to see the manager, Gary, counting money and looking exhausted. The office had a claustrophobic, attic-like feel to it—there was a musty rug and the smell of cigarettes.

I tried my greeting again, figuring that was my chance to get the ball rolling. He looked over at me and said, "I'll be with you in a bit." I wasn't sure what to make of that. He gave me a look of indifference. *What period of time would be "in a bit?" Should I find something to keep me busy? Should I stand here at attention? Is there somewhere else I should wait?*

The office was a decent size, but it was loaded with merchandise, old racks, and employee coats and bags with no visible waiting area. I felt if I continued to just stand here, I would be breathing down his neck. The next two or three minutes were excruciatingly awkward. *Enough of this,* I thought. "I'll be downstairs waiting and get familiar with the store," I told him. I thought making this move would break the ice, but I got nothing back. Bupkis. Not even the universal slight head nod to signify he heard my voice. Down the stairs I went, feeling relief to get away from that awkward attic.

As I navigated the narrow aisles, mixing in with the customers shopping, I was having one of those moments of doubt. Parking would cost me $100 per week and I had about $500 in the bank. The greeting here was cold at best and I was sleeping on a porch. Maybe I didn't think this whole Boston thing through.

But I stiffened up as I dismissed the doubts in my mind. That would not be helpful in working though my first day. I needed to be determined and show a strong sense of confidence that I'm here and ready for work. This was now my home and going back was not an option. Once I made that decision, I thought of the metaphor for leaving home in the song Ice Fishing by Bill Morrisey:

And there ain't much to ice fishing
Till you're gone a day or more
And the hole you've cut freezes over
And it's like you've never been there before

No turning back now, the hole back home is frozen over, and change sometimes comes with its share of challenges. I decided, in order to work off these nervous jitters and moments of self-doubt, I would get busy.

I walked the store and quickly turned on my manager instincts. I found my way into the cooler and began stocking the shelves. *I got this*, I thought—the greeting I received today wasn't like John's "Thomas, my friend, how are you?" But maybe I just caught them at a busy moment.

Gary finally found me and brought me upstairs. "I need your help," he said in a low, almost defeated tone. He looked exhausted and stressed. "Sure, what's up?" At this point, I felt a bit of sympathy for him. What he shared next was not what I was expecting. "I need you to cover some shifts for me. I'm short on help and haven't had a day off for weeks." Wait, I was told I was going to get training to be a manager and take over my own store in about four weeks. What was I going to say? I felt like he really needed some relief.

"OK—what shift did you need me to cover?"

"Midnight shifts, tonight, and the rest of the week," was his reply and not at all what I was expecting to hear.

I quickly pushed aside the fact that I needed to be back at the store the same night to work the overnight shift and turned to more practical matters. I wanted his guidance on parking since I knew that was not a sustainable expense. "Why did you drive and park there?" he said looking at me dumbfounded. "Because it's just over there across the street," I said. "Take the green line, the station is right down the street," he replied.

I later learned the "green line" was the subway. My first day. Working midnights. Downtown. Riding the subway. I'm truly in a brave new world here. But I rolled with it.

The subway was an experience to me all on its own. In Buffalo, the only public transportation were the city busses, and most parking was abundant and free. I arrived at the subway stop closest to my house to embark on a new adventure. The subway station had a large board with the map of the entire system on it. What looked like a very structured, green, red, blue, silver diagram of how to ride the subway left me thinking simply, "This looks great, but how do I get to work?" The map didn't answer that. I also learned walking up to strangers in the subway station and asking questions would only get you blank stares and cold shoulders.

But, like everything else, I found my way. I conquered the subway system and worked those midnight shifts. I also got proper orientation and training at the Copley store and finally got my own store to manage in Charlestown. It was just a few miles from my place in Somerville—and they had a parking lot! Things were looking up!

The store was located in Thompson Square in the historic town where the battle of Bunker Hill was fought in 1775. I fell in love when I walked into the store. It just felt good. Really good.

Mark, the manager, was behind the counter when I walked in. This time, I received a warm smile and a gregarious hello. We were relatively close in age, mid-20s at the time. Mark was a singer in a rock band. He had long black hair and could often be found performing in the local Allston/Boston music scene. Mark had a big personality and was as genuine as they come. He was in the midst of writing the schedule and I noticed he wrote his name across all seven days from midnight to 8 a.m. "Are you training someone?" I asked. "Didn't they tell you; we have no midnight help here, they just quit," he said. "I'm going to work this week, then you are on your own." He had a big smile on his face, which was not meant to be disrespectful, but rather, "I'm tired—glad you are taking over."

Here we go, back on midnights. Finding help that summer of 1986 was difficult to say the least. A booming economy was keeping people employed elsewhere and working overnight shifts in Charlestown was not at the top of everyone's list of dream jobs. But I found some relief during this summer of long overnight shifts —along with a friend I will never forget.

Tom Brown was a part-time member of the team who had two other jobs. He drove a bus, worked as a janitor, and worked at the store in his spare time. He didn't want to be on the schedule, but rather help out when we were in dire straits. Tom was a tall and powerful looking man, somewhat intimidating if you didn't know he had a kind, warm heart, and a boisterous sense of humor. He was a gentle giant really.

Tom also had a heavy Boston accent. I'm talking the really thick Boston accent that people often attribute to President John F. Kennedy. Tom was someone who was tired but strong. Determined and honest. The kind of person who, if you had them in your corner, would make life a bit more special.

Tom would stop in almost every night to spend some time with me. He grew up in Charlestown and knew almost everyone who walked in the front door. Eventually I became the guy who was a friend of Tom's—which helped give me some credibility with the townies. In fact, most of my team was born and raised in Charlestown. It was like having your stronger big brother with you when he was around. When any troublemakers walked through the front door, the sight of Tom behind the counter kind of kept everyone in line.

Tom would stop by and give me a break to grab something to eat, or get a jump start on my paperwork. His signature phrase was "Go on, screw," before taking over the register for me. At first, I wasn't sure how to interpret this phrase. But I came to know it simply meant I could go do some other work or take a break for a while. I remember thinking, *If I'm lucky enough to have a family one day, I want to be like Tom.* He was a hard worker who was dedicated to his family and making sure they had what they needed.

I recall vividly the day a few years into managing the store I received a phone call that would shake me to my core. I was now married with two kids. My wife told me our daughter Gillian had been in a car accident and was on the way to the hospital with a head injury. The doctors were concerned with swelling of the brain. I immediately felt a rush of panic go through my body. If I hadn't been sitting, I may have collapsed right there.

Tom happened to stop by for a coffee that day and was at the end of the counter. I announced to the team working what had happened and said I would be leaving immediately. Tom could sense I was panicked and walked with me to my car. He said, "Let me drive you to the hospital." I replied no, I can do it, my voice cracking a bit. I got behind the wheel and started the car. He stuck his head in the car, grabbed me by the shirt and said, "Take a breath. You won't do your family any good by you getting in an accident too. If you won't let me drive, promise you'll take it easy." He gave me a stare that only Tom could muster up. Our eyes connected for about 10 seconds. I took a breath, centered myself and assured him, I would follow his advice. "Now get outta here and go be with your family," he said. "We got the store covered."

After a few frightful hours, Gillian would recover and be fine. The next time I saw Tom, I thanked him for settling me down. "So the girl, your daughter, she gonna be ok?" he asked in his rough Boston accent. "Yeah, she will," I replied. As he turned and said "That's good," I saw a big smile on his face, joining me in the relief that she would be ok.

Tom had an abundance of grit to be sure, but a kind, warm heart made him a very special person, and I'm glad to have had him in my life. I will treasure each of those moments with Tom. I think the people you meet and share vulnerable moments with never really leave you. I'm thankful for that.

So, I worked midnights pretty much the entire summer. But Tom made it a little easier to bear. The overnight faces became familiar, and I looked forward to seeing them.

My Moment of Reflection

It's these seemingly chaotic experiences that created memorable friendships and tested my grit—which only made me more determined to persevere. Embracing these hardships in my life also inspired me to keep moving and forge new ways ahead.

My not-so-welcome orientation on my first week

at Store 24 inspired me years later to lead a team to create training programs that focused on driving success for employees starting with their first day on the job. The memory of me standing in that office, feeling like I was invisible or a bother, made me determined to make people feel welcome when they began their journey with us. These efforts ultimately improved our retention and employee satisfaction. By placing an emphasis on the first few hours on the job, people were now staying with the company longer. It shows how early impressions can form their opinions and potentially send them in a different direction or ignite a fire in them to learn more. Showing you care and are invested in their future carries a significant weight in how willing they are to be all-in on the team's future efforts.

Working midnights would open a new view of the world I never would have experienced without this opportunity, which at the time seemed like a hardship. There's something special that takes place during the night when most people are sleeping. I watched a cascading change, observing how the world woke up and shook off the previous day to start anew. During the first part of the night, there would be the people that may be up later than they should and perhaps headed for mischief. But you would also get the people getting off their shift, picking up a sandwich before they headed home at the end of a long day. Then there were the early risers who were headed to work, getting their coffee before the local shops were even open.

Of course, the police and other first responders would be in and out throughout the night. Bo, a veteran Boston police officer, stopped in most nights for coffee and to see how I was doing. Bobby, who always had a big smile and something nice to say, dropped off the bundles of newspapers inside the front door around 3 a.m. He would yell greetings across the store, always with a huge smile, and be on his way. And of course, the small group of older gentlemen hanging around the front door would descend on those bundles like there was earth-shattering breaking news to absorb. But ultimately, they just wanted to be paired with a cup of coffee, read the sports page, and banter about the Celtics—taking part in a routine you could tell was practiced for decades. Marjorie, my favorite customer, would stop in every day around 4 a.m. like clockwork to wipe down the counters and brew coffee for me. She loved helping and never wanted a job, she just loved helping people.

It was a special time each night, witnessing this community of people prepare the world so it was ready for everyone else to finally wake from their slumber, hours later, and begin their day. They had a common bond without a spoken word amongst them. It was a look in their eyes I got to know and love. The coffee would be made, the newspapers ready; we were there to help in some small way to get them started. I learned a lot from those midnight shifts and will forever remember the people I met.

As far as sleeping on the porch, I was fortunate to have a safe place to sleep and keep my belongings. Riding the subway and walking the streets of Boston I became acutely aware of the challenges of homelessness in the city. I was grateful to live with friends and have a hot meal whenever I wanted. That's not to say what I experienced wasn't challenging, but I persevered and put any setbacks behind me. Experiences are part of who you are, but it's how you embrace these moments as you go through life that can make the difference in future outcomes.

Tom Brown gave me comfort. The porch gave me shelter. The late-night community let me be part of their world. I'm grateful for every experience. Every person. Every moment.

Chapter 4

Leadership Lessons From My Team

"Life is all about creating special moments. In the end, only these special moments will matter."

—Purvi Raniga

During the next seven years, I used my experience as a store manager to take on the responsibilities of district manager. A few years after that, I was promoted to being a regional manager. This wasn't career planning in action. Rather, a new challenge was put before me, and I would accept it. I was married with two kids now, and this seemed to be a natural path for me to follow. Truth be told, the district manager position first appealed to me since it came with a company car. My car was slowly preparing itself for retirement and money was tight, so I jumped at the offer.

One of my biggest challenges came soon after. I was offered the job as Director of Operations. The company had many challenges before them, and everything seemed to funnel back through operations. Did I really want to be that central person in the company where all problems ended up on my doorstep? Several people before me had not succeeded in the job and it seemed risky. I had a family and needed stability. This weighed on me at the time, but also seemed to nudge me in the direction of accepting the job. Not that I ever considered saying no, but mentally I shifted from uncertainty to "I got this."

So, I took on the responsibilities as Director of Operations in 1995. It felt right, and I felt ready.

There were a few of us that got to the office quite early. I'm sure it was a continuation of the routine I picked up from my father back when I would arrive with him at Trico Plant #1 an hour and a half before my shift started. I had about an hour-long commute, so getting in early had the added benefit of avoiding sitting in traffic. I enjoyed the commute and realized it was the perfect time to think through the challenges I was heading into for the day. We didn't have cellphones at the time, so driving inside your car was an opportunity to shut out the world and have time to think. We did have pagers though, and all that did was send your stress level sky high until you could make an exit and find a payphone or wait until your next stop to call in.

One particular morning, the rain was beating down on my windshield with intensity as I made my familiar way along the Mass Pike. My mother had recently passed, and as I made my exit off the highway, I remember wondering what she would have thought about these new responsibilities.

My conversations on the phone when I was a store manager with my parents went something like this - almost every time:

My father:
How's the store going?
How's the car running?
You saving some money?
Here's your mother.

My mother:
How are you feeling?
You're getting older, you going to settle down?
(Translation: Will you be getting married soon?)
You going to church every Sunday?
Do you think you will ever come back to Buffalo to live?
Your father wants to say goodbye (she yells into the next room).

Not exactly every time, but almost. I had my answers down pat. The store was going great, my car had a tank of gas and was running, I had a few hundred dollars in the bank, I felt good, someday, avoided answering, and no, I'm not moving back.

I was in the midst of a generational shift. As the youngest in the family, I was taking a direction they didn't understand. Moving out of state, away from the neighborhood where my family lived and working in an unconventional job in their mind didn't seem to make sense. But their worry came from loving hearts and wanting the best for their son. So I never let that bother me.

Eventually, after my mother passed, my father changed the opening question to: *How's it going with "the stores?" Do you go out and make sure things are ok?*

I don't think he really understood the job, not many people do, but he was pleased to see me taking on more responsibility. He added two questions once I was married and had kids:

Don't work so hard that it affects your health. You taking time off?
How's the family? Say hello to Barbara (my wife).

As I arrived at the office and pulled into the parking lot, I seemed to be keenly aware that morning of the sounds around me. As I turned in the parking lot, the crunch of the loose gravel under my tires seemed to announce my arrival, and my shoes clacking on the wet pavement broke the quiet security of the warm, dry car and introduced the harsh realities of the day. Walking towards the front door, the entryway to where it all begins each day, was like crossing a threshold. I felt a noticeable shift from lingering on my meandering thoughts on the commute to snapping into an instant focus as the day's events were about to unfold.

I reached my office on the second floor and continued to hear the rain falling in the quietness of the moment—I took some inspiration hearing the raindrops tapping on my windowpane, bouncing off the roof. Is the rain washing away the challenges of the past or bringing new life to the situation at hand? Perhaps both might be true, I hoped.

As a store manager, district manager, and even regional manager, I had colleagues to commiserate with and share frustrations through the usual camaraderie that comes with carrying out similar responsibilities. Sitting in my office alone seemed to highlight the feeling of singularity of the decisions at times. You get input of course, but then the room goes silent as you hand out the final call. It's kind of like in football. If the quarterback throws the ball on 4th down on the one-yard line and connects for a touchdown, no one questions the decision— "Brilliant, exactly what I would have done!" the fans would exclaim. But an incomplete pass meant a lonely walk through the tunnel. "What a horrible call," would be the hot take on every Monday morning talk show.

Managing operations means every day will create a challenge. I had to shift my mindset from, "Why are you bringing me problems?" to "Let's solve this together." That did not come easy.

I knew small changes wouldn't have the kind of breakthrough results we needed. I recently approached the Chief Operating Officer about a new structure. What if we could start over from scratch? If we were starting a new company tomorrow, what kind of operations team would we put in place knowing what we know today? The previous week I put together a completely new team structure to propose. We would eliminate district managers and create teams.

Each team would have a leader, merchandising manager, people manager and operations manager. They would have a lot more stores, but a more focused approach. We would also tie in the facilities person to round out the team. I walked into Steve's office, laid the plans for restructuring on his desk and said, "I want to implement this plan. Next week." He previously liked the idea, but gave me a look that seemed to say, "Are you sure?" That surprised me and for a split second I thought "Am I?" I quickly erased that thought and replied, "100 percent."

We brought it to the executive team, and they signed off. We created new positions with HR and several promotions were about to be announced. I pulled together my operations team and unveiled the plan. "We are creating new teams and you will all have targeted responsibilities. This will share the burden of the day's issues and create a new way of operating." I shared all of the details of this groundbreaking adventure we were about to take together with a pride and excitement I hadn't felt before. The feeling wasn't mutual.

Dead silence. This was not the reaction I was expecting. Blank stares, simmering anger, no positive energy whatsoever and mine was slowly being sucked out of me. I just took on a new role, restructured the department, and everyone was looking directly at me like I broke it. I was now a bit back on my heels and becoming defensive. I knew what we were doing wasn't working and we needed to make changes. I was certain they felt the same way. What I didn't consider was that most people loved their current role. They worked hard to get there. They were being pulled away from being the leader of their team. Now they are part of this larger team and that seemed to be a step back. After much explaining back and forth, the reality that this was the path forward settled in for the team. We focused on implementing and announcing the changes to the rest of the company. But instead of this new idea infusing new energy into our day, we were plodding through the details. The rain felt like it wasn't nourishing new life, but rather hanging a gray cloud over us.

The afternoon went smoother since we were meeting with the individuals being promoted. These discussions energized me. I saw the excitement in their eyes as they were being recognized for their hard work and a new career was opened before them. Perhaps this excitement would also energize the team and we would move on quickly.

It wasn't as simple as that. I hadn't thought through every single scenario that would play out in the coming months. That was a mistake. Anticipating the unintended consequences should have been part of my planning, but it wasn't. They were right to call me out on it. Later that day I was peppered with legit questions, but a little bit like, "Hey, Mr. Know It All, who has ultimate authority? Should I not deal with issues I discover when it is not my 'area of focus?'" No doubt, some of the questions were meant to throw water on the entire plan, but I tried to listen and not overreact to their frustrations. In fact, they were great questions when I was objective about it.

After the meeting and feedback session, I headed back to my office and closed the door. Several thoughts were running through my mind. *Did I move too fast? Had I just unleashed a slow-moving train that would run off the track?*

As I looked out my office window, the rain had stopped, and the sun was breaking from behind the clouds. I spotted two members of the team standing in the middle of the parking lot, deep in conversation. One newly promoted, the other a seasoned supervisor. As they finished the conversation, I could see they both flashed warm smiles and a nod, as if to say "Looking forward to working with you." I may have been reading too much into it, but I realized, I'm looking at this the wrong way. This restructure was my idea, but I needed the team to help me make it a success. An idea alone, even when implemented does not magically become successful. For this to work, I needed the team to want this to succeed as much as I did. They were a bright, talented group of people that I put in place with new responsibilities, and I needed to lead.

The entire new team was now together in our conference room. First, I admitted that I didn't think through every scenario and needed their help in resolving them. This didn't mean I was second guessing my decision. Any fleeting moments of doubt were gone, and I felt resolved. I knew they needed to see that in me, but also share that I needed their help in making the plans successful. As I looked around the table, I felt a deep sense of pride. We had been through a lot together over the years and I knew I could always count on them. They were upset because they care, and they love their job. We started tossing out different scenarios we would need to handle. One team member started documenting the key points and we were off and running!

Next, I shared my vision that this is an opportunity for them to see the job in a new light. I expected new ideas, changes in how we operate – nothing is sacred. Let's take the mindset used to create this new structure. *What if we could start over from scratch? If we were starting a new company tomorrow, what kind of operations structure would we put in place knowing what we know today?* Except in this case, we were discussing how we can be most effective in this new team environment. They were sharing ideas and I could see the team starting to settle in and leaning into the idea of how they can support each other's efforts. This is the perfect time for a leader to say little, and let your team take the reins.

Lastly, I let them know I should have considered how these changes would have affected them personally. It was a learning experience for me, and I would use it for future planning. They may not like every future decision, or change. But we were a team, and we have an opportunity to have breakthrough results together. I felt a shift in the room. It's not "I got this" it's "*We* got this." A gritty, determined bunch they were, and I was fortunate to be part of their team.

My Moment of Reflection

I learned many life lessons that week. I was determined to move forward and had no plans to reverse course. It's what we needed; I was sure of that. But, as a leader you need to share your vulnerabilities and areas where you need help, especially in the most difficult of circumstances. In fact, it's precisely those times you need a team effort. Sparking the idea, creating disruption, and making critical changes are the beginning. But listening, asking questions, and learning from your team are where you achieve success.

I also tucked away in my memory the look on everyone's faces as we revealed our plans. They hadn't been part of the discussion and we were shifting them away from a position they loved. It's clear a leader must make these decisions and can't buckle because some on the team will disagree. But understanding that empathy is part of the job cannot be overstated. Sharing that you know this may be difficult for them to accept, but you need their help to fuel the company's future success.

The other lesson I learned was that big changes can lead to breakthrough results. It wasn't that financial results soared and every metric immediately surpassed expectation. But we provided new career opportunities, unleashed new skills and the ideas, and changes in how we operate made us a better company out into the future.

Now, I'd like the ending to that story to be that this type of structure revolutionized the industry and became a model for all. That's not the ending though. After about 18 months, we reverted back to a traditional district manager role. It wasn't because it failed, although at first glance, that might be the perception. We had grown as a team, changed the way we approached the business, and were now ready to shift back into our previous structure, almost. We created a new merchandising team and an operations manager. If I could go back in time, would I still move ahead with the same plan? The simple answer is yes, but I would have used the lessons I learned. I don't think we would have achieved the same results with small changes. We needed a boost in our creativity and a way to shake us out of our comfort zones. I think we all learned a lot during that time. I certainly did and relied on those lessons throughout my life.

Leadership involves passion and perseverance. My team had those qualities, and I could not have been prouder of them. I felt fortunate to lead such a team, at a time when we needed their dedication and determination to succeed.

They were my inspiration to do my best at work. That is a life moment in which I'll be forever grateful.

Chapter 5

Believe in Yourself

"One important key to success is self-confidence. An important key to self-confidence is preparation."

—Arthur Ashe

I had several months under my belt as Director of Operations when it became time for my first address to the company in this role. We typically held managers' meetings twice a year, where managers from 90 stores across New England would get together for a full day of seminars and team-building sessions. I would give the final wrap-up speech to synthesize key points and send everyone off feeling inspired by the day's events.

Tall order. Especially for someone who is an introvert by nature and typically looking for the politest way and earliest time to find an exit in any social event I've ever attended. I've always felt most comfortable working in a conference room or in the field, problem-solving with the team, not in front of 100-plus people staring back at me.

I was sitting at my desk, thinking maybe my nerves stem back to fifth grade when Sister Mary Michael would have each student read a paragraph aloud from a schoolbook in science class. I dreaded when my turn came around. She would always announce each student's name in dramatic fashion, which I found a bit peculiar and distracting from the chapter's subject matter. "Mister Gavin!" "Miss Harrigan!" she'd shout. When it was time to fill the room with my voice and deliver prose about Nicolaus Copernicus or photosynthesis, she belted out, "Mister Hart!" She tilted her head down and peered at me over the top of her glasses. I'm not sure she ever used our first name for whatever reason, with a slight pause in-between the Mister and Hart. If you got stuck on a word, she would announce loudly, "Sound it out, Mister Hart." We would read out loud for what seemed to be hours on end. I always felt a sense of relief and I might say, accomplishment, getting through my fifth-grade oratory responsibilities.

Drifting back to the present moment I started to internalize the same self-doubt. What if I completely botched my first attempt? Would I get another chance? Would a poor performance mark me with a lack of credibility? What would I have to add to the day that would provide my team inspiration? What if Sister Mary Michael popped into my head in that moment and I froze like I was sitting in row three, seat two in science class?

My way of compensating for a lack of confidence was preparation. Really preparing, as in countless hours of practice, research, planning, and you guessed it, more practice. I learned early in my life practice is a skill, or discipline, that you can give yourself every day. Any time I've taken a task for granted it typically does not go well. I think having the opportunity to manage a store for quite a few years helped me understand the importance of planning and preparation.

As far as the secret to my research for speeches and many other initiatives in the business, sometimes it was as simple as talking to the right people. My go-to person for a "What's on people's minds" perspective was John Mahoney, a seasoned store manager. I could get a quick pulse of morale or get his honest feedback on something I was working on. So, I packed up a few things and made a stop by John's store, which would be my last task for the day. It was about a 25-minute drive from the office, so I poured the last of the burnt coffee sitting in the bottom of the glass pot from the office kitchen and I was on my way. Quality and taste weren't the priority at the moment, just a bit of caffeine to get me through the final part of the day.

I always had the same feeling arriving at one of our stores—renewed appreciation for an incredibly challenging job. While we were in the office planning, meeting, and creating new ways to run our business, the stores always operated 24 hours a day, 365 days a year. As I opened the front door, I could sense the hustle and bustle of employees and customers moving about the store, with fresh coffee brewing along with the familiar aroma of a microwaved burrito or burger. His store never stopped radiating energy.

Whenever I visited him, I knew I had to share my time with the customers and employees as his head was always on a swivel – "Hey Susan, good to see you!" "Tom, I need to help up front, be right back" or "Can we talk over here so I can wipe down the coffee counter?" He would often break away in mid-sentence, but pick right back up where he left off. As people gave John a shout out to say hello and at times, they would give me a serious look as if to say, "I got your back John, this guy bothering you?" I would just smile, impressed by how much they cared for him. I remember the day we went down the street for lunch. The owner of the restaurant and most of the customers all knew him by name and flashed big smiles as they noticed him. It was like having lunch with a celebrity!

My visits with John were not to collect names, or specific details that would break his trust with others, but to give me an honest assessment of what was on their minds—good and bad. I genuinely wanted to know the truth, the whole truth and nothing but the truth. Specifically, if you had to choose the one topic that you think I need to address—what would it be? John said that morale was actually pretty good, and people were excited about many of the changes we put into place. But they wanted to be more involved and have an opportunity to be part of the process. They had ideas but weren't sure how to advance them. That's fair I thought, and a healthy place to be. The lifeblood of the organization were the people serving the customer, so getting their ideas would be instrumental to our success.

As John continued to share his insights, I started to think about more than just sharing ideas. What if we involved them early on about what's on our mind, during the initial stages of our planning? That could be a powerful formula for a true partnership with the people we depended on day in and day out to deliver results. We chatted about a few other things going on and I thanked John for his time, and more importantly his candidness. He probably thought nothing of it, but it was something I really treasured and over time, became a better leader because of our conversations. Simply put, I learned a lot from John Mahoney.

I started my drive home, and the planning began. My research for this particular speech was complete. John helped me get my messaging settled and now it's time for preparation. My dog Misty, always by my side in my office at home, would have to endure a few hours of me preparing my remarks. She was the perfect dog really. A rescue lab shepherd mix who had an energy that was endless. I remember the day we adopted Misty, we had an apartment at the time and needed the landlord's approval. He gave us his blessing and off we went to the rescue to bring home a new member of the family. As we approached the yard where the dogs were kept, it was heartbreaking. The fenced-in area had about a dozen dogs, and they all seemed to want to come home with us. But one dog in particular stuck her nose through the chain link fence as if she was trying to break through and jump into our car. She was a beautiful, black, mostly lab-looking girl. My heart melted at that moment. I looked at Barbara and the kids, and without saying a word, we knew it was unanimous, "We would like to adopt her." Off we went as she jumped into the backseat of the car. We drove off with that fresh wet dog smell filling the car. It was a perfect moment. She instantly acted like she had been a member of the family forever, jumping around the backseat with both kids and at times trying to wiggle her way up front to give everyone a sloppy kiss. It was almost like she was saying, "Thank you, thank you, thank you!" and probably "What's for dinner?"

It was slightly raining that day, so we settled on the name Misty, to be forever tied to that moment we met. She would soon get quite a few more friends when we bought a home, growing to a pack of five dogs running through a 1,300-square-foot home, and later a horse named Joe who lived in a barn in the backyard. But Misty was the boss, and she knew it, in a kind, but assertive way.

Whenever she was in the room, she brought a

joy to my heart and a comfort to my soul that is hard to describe. Whether she was often running around, bouncing off the back of the couch or curled up, sleeping in my chair, she was my girl. We were best friends really, for 16 years. As I practiced my remarks, she lifted her head at one point as if to say, "You got this." I guess it also could have been, "I'm trying to sleep, enough already," but I went with– "You got this." I agreed – I got this.

The next morning, as I was driving to the hotel where we were holding the meeting, I had a deep sense of pride thinking about all the planning that took place to bring this event together. The event would bring together 90 store managers and around 50 people from the support center for a day of learning and team building. Those are some of the best bonding and learning moments in life–getting ready for something special. Seeing the team begin to discuss a possible idea rather quietly, then people build on it and their eyes ignite as it came alive. That moment when Idea after idea started to flow, some gentle ribbing when we would veer too far off into the creative process, endless energy starting to fill the room, people now out of their chairs pacing about the conference table and all of the sudden you have created something very special. Those life moments are a gift that become beautiful to open from time to time.

My peers were second to no one I thought – this would be a great day together. The day unfolded exactly as planned. The mood was positive, and I felt a sense of excitement from the managers. Working in an environment, serving the public, 24/7 is a lot of stress on an individual. Getting out with your peers, in a completely different environment had a way of de-stressing them for the day and allowing them to enjoy a new experience. Many had been up since pre-dawn to get their paperwork done before they attended the meeting. But they didn't show their weariness, or at least they hid it well.

As everyone settled in their seats, finishing up quick conversations before turning their attention to an end of day wrap-up. It was at that moment the room became silent. It was like everyone was saying with their silence and staring straight ahead, "let's go up front – what do you have to say?"

I decided to breakdown my remarks into three areas that day:

- Inform
- Inspire
- Include

First, I wanted to address several initiatives we recently developed and deployed and how they would be impacted - inform. We needed to act with a renewed sense of energy and blaze a new trail. I wanted everyone to know I had confidence in our decisions and more importantly our people. I shared how this new direction would shape our future and build towards a better tomorrow together.

Next, I wanted to inspire the group about the importance of their role. All of our planning for the future is dependent on the store teams they manage. The decisions they make every day to hire the right people, coach their teams, keeping them motivated and energized is essential to our future success. They decide each day who will represent us to the customer. That responsibility should come with a sense of pride and determination to be the best. Surround yourself with people who want to succeed and go above and beyond. I certainly knew that, as my team inspired me to do my best each day.

The third area I needed to communicate was inclusion. We would be formalizing a key manager group to represent the field to be involved in future planning, provide feedback, and be proactive in solving problems that leadership didn't have visibility into. I needed their partnership in bringing to life our vision of building a better tomorrow.

Inform, inspire, and inclusion seemed to fit the bill that day. As I finished my remarks, I remember being filled with a deep sense of appreciation as I looked out amongst the people in the room. I drew my energy from their positivity and excitement.

We adjourned for the day, and the managers began to shuffle towards the hotel lounge. You could see the servers and bartenders preparing for the rush of guests and soon the room would be filled with a familiar aroma of chicken wings, nachos, and burgers as everyone shared some laughter, swapped stories of challenging times and got caught up with family updates–this one graduated from high school, another is off to college or their current move to a new place. This was an opportunity to share a few moments with their peers they don't often get to see, whom they shared a bond with that was clearly visible on their faces. These moments were comforting to witness as the room began to fill with voices, clanging dishes and people sharing a meal together. I always relished in the satisfaction that came from the conclusion of events like today.

I could sense a change was in the air. We were all headed in a new direction. I think it's something we all wanted. We *needed*. So the journey on a new path began. There was work ahead to be sure, but we were ready. This was our moment.

My Moment of Reflection

I made my way home that night to reflect on the day's event. As I passed the familiar rest stops filled with weary travelers I thought about the day and what would be ahead of me. I was really proud of how far we had come as a team. We had been through a lot of difficult days and taking time to dream a bit, laugh together, and share ideas is important to people who get dragged into the nitty gritty of each day. That happens to all of us in life. The changes we plan to make can get left on the back burner if we get lost in the day-to-day focus. I learned from experience, especially in my new role, that you must deal with the immediate needs decisively or you would get crushed in the oncoming challenges. But you also need to keep an eye towards the future, or you get stuck in the present. It was a delicate balance, harmonized with learning and experience. No doubt someone will walk through my door tomorrow with a problem we will need to hash out. It could be one of those days where difficult conversations will occupy the day. But I was determined to keep an eye focused on the future during even the most difficult of times. It was expected of me as a leader. I was determined to keep this promise of balance to the team.

I also learned not to underestimate myself. Leave that for others to do–they had, and they will in the future. I can't be concerned with that. I learned that confidence is a skill you can nurture over time. My early lack of confidence was bolstered by preparation. So can yours!

It's important to understand what confidence is and is not.

Confidence is not:

- Thinking you are better than others
- Being the most talented in the room
- Making others feel inferior by exclusion

Confidence is:

- Admitting when you are wrong
- Having people on your team who can replace you

- Asking questions when you don't understand something
- Giving others credit, often and genuinely

We went on to form a group of key managers who I would meet with monthly. I learned so much from them at every meeting. I would hear some hard truths that sometimes would feel like a slap on the back of the head. Something you weren't expecting. But if I weren't here with them, they would be having the same discussions, but without me. I remember vividly the day we created a bonus program for managers and their team with about two hours of back and forth discussion, giving and taking, until we finally settled on something we all agreed was fair and exciting. We would continue to have great conversations, laugh a bit, share some pizza, and build a special bond I will carry with me forever. *This group helps me believe in myself*, I thought, as I grabbed a slice of pepperoni. For these moments with them, I'm truly grateful.

Chapter 6

A Disastrous Performance,
A Gift of a Lifetime

"Courage doesn't always roar. Sometimes courage is the little voice at the end of the day that says I'll try again tomorrow."

—Mary Anne Radmacher

I gazed out my office window into the darkness of a particularly cold February night. It was the winter of 1997, and I had taken the position of Vice President of Store 24. I was still working with operations, but now guided marketing as well. We had frigid weather for weeks and it was the time of year in New England when most people leave before sunrise and return home after sunset. I only saw my house in the daylight on weekends. It was a long day, and I needed to muster a second wind to attend a meeting in Boston scheduled for 7 p.m. We were asked to attend a regularly scheduled neighborhood meeting and I hadn't given much thought as to why, but this was part of the responsibility of operating in cities like Boston.

Knowing I wouldn't be having dinner that night, I took a quick swing by the office kitchen area to see if there was something I could grab to eat along the way. I picked through the mound of assorted snacks on top of the counter, looking for something that could resemble dinner when I spotted my meal for the night—beef jerky. Perfect. Dinner was served. I headed down to my car, sitting in a mostly empty lot by now, and headed downtown, into the night.

As I drove along the highway my mind drifted back to a typical winter's day in Buffalo as a store manager. Everything was a bit more challenging in the winter season. Delivery trucks would bring in the ice and snow, making it a full-time job to keep the floors dry. Delivery drivers seemed to be in a constant state of exhaustion as they trudged through the day. Driving, lifting, wheeling, and stacking in the summer was one thing; working with snow and ice was another.

One day back in Buffalo in the winter of 1979, John asked me to give Ron, the RC Cola driver, a hand. He always had a pained look on his face, one that bore the scars of backbreaking work for many years. His face was ruddy, and he wore giant gloves that were too big and a hat that was always a bit crooked. He could never really stand upright and walked with a bit of a limp. This job seemed to be a poor fit for someone in his condition, but I guess it was a matter of what he has been doing most of his life and it became his way to earn a living. He never complained, not once.

In those days, the crates were wooden, and the bottles were glass. Ron's crates were wobbly, and always about to come apart as the nails pulled away from the corners. I started to make it a routine to give Ron a hand each time. I would drop whatever I was doing and head out to the truck. "Let me help today, Ron," I said. He always had a smile on his face and thanked me a dozen times as we would haul in the delivery.

I came to really respect what Ron did day in and day out. Ron had grit and I looked forward to his weekly stops. We'd banter back and forth while helping each other out. Our friendship grew over time, and our connection always left me with a warm feeling whenever we shared an experience. He was the kind of man who looked directly into your heart and soul when he said thanks and showed appreciation. I think I appreciated our time together more than the actual crate lifting, but the ritual of stacking and unstacking together came with the territory. Delivery people can sometimes be taken for granted. I always found them to be interesting people to get to know, and Ron was one of those I will never forget.

Back to that night in 1997, I made my way down the neighborhood street close to the meeting. I circled the block to find a parking space as I started to focus on what the meeting agenda would be tonight. Finding parking in Boston was a bit of an acquired skill, and required a boatload of patience. Plus, being arguably the world's worst parallel parker, my options were limited. I finally found my spot, about two blocks from the meeting hall.

The cold brought me to attention quickly as I stepped out of the car. It was one of those nights where you could actually smell the frigid air. It's the kind of scent that's hard to put into words— a cold crispness—but if you have ever lived in temperatures that settled somewhere below 20 degrees for long periods of time, you know what I mean. Walking the sidewalks in any winter city keeps you focused on avoiding the patches of black ice, stepping over snowbanks with care. My pair of dress shoes with zero traction were no help—my choice of footwear was perhaps an indication I didn't fully prepare for this event. The frigid wind whipping against my face could have been another signal for the chilly reception I was about to encounter.

I entered the meeting room to a full house mixed with neighbors, Boston Police, and some civic leaders. I immediately felt like an outsider. I got that feeling you get when you walk into a room and everyone goes silent, turns, and looks in your direction. Kind of like that. The aroma of coffee mixed with the cold air coming in from outside filled the room as everyone started to find their seats.

The people attending a neighborhood meeting are there with a goal of making their community a safer place to live and enhancing the overall quality of life. They were often arriving at the end of a long day at work too, which meant there was a laser-like focus from the crowd during the two hours (or more) devoted to the meetings.

We were on the agenda, there to listen to concerns and introduce ourselves to the neighborhood. But our turn was further down the list—last specifically. The people speaking before me were really in tune with the neighborhood. They were reading from notes, calling on people by name, and referencing follow-up items from the last meeting. I hadn't received all the usual updates, and worse, didn't recognize any familiar faces. As we moved down the agenda, I could sense an impending feeling of doom. Suddenly the cold outdoor air seemed like the warmest place to be right now in comparison to taking center stage.

Soon, we were up and I made my way to the front of the room. The other speakers had left which almost made me feel a bit abandoned. It's like they rushed out because they knew what was coming and didn't want to be part of any collateral damage.

I stood in front of the crowd, introduced myself, and began to speak to the crowd and listen to their concerns. Let me tell you: I got absolutely crushed. We heard about rowdy crowds gathering in the parking lot late at night, poor lighting in and around the store, loud truck deliveries at 3 a.m. that woke up the neighborhood, and a lack of steady attendance at this meeting.

According to the locals, we were not adding to the quality of life in the neighborhood. In fact, we were making it worse. They felt we didn't care—which was the opposite of my intention. By the end of the meeting, I felt like I was responsible for everything that went wrong in the neighborhood. They hated me. I hated me. So, I stammered, took notes and left the room, tail between my legs and a bit shaken. How did I let it get to this point?

I began my walk to the car as the cold air, its unforgiving wind slapping me in the face as if to say, "I warned you." We were all pouring out into the street at the same time. Many of those locals likely hadn't had dinner yet, worked a long day, and had their family waiting at home. I just wanted to escape into the quietness of my car and start heading home myself. I could sense the people walking around me as they too parked down the street a bit, many were close enough to walk home from the meeting.

My mind was racing as I fumbled for my keys, car in sight. As I went to unlock the door, I must have hit the car alarm and the sudden noise coming from my car was piercing. Not just to my ears, but everyone around me. Here I was disturbing the neighborhood, right after they told me we were disturbing the neighborhood. As all eyes turned towards me as I fumbled with the door, alarm screaming into the quietness of

the night. All I could think of was, you have got
to be kidding me.

I could feel the people around me staring, most
likely thinking "Is that the same putz we just
heard from at the meeting?" I got the alarm to
finally stop. I quickly stepped into my car and
shut the door. The silence was deafening. Well,
that could not have gone worse. I sat there for a
few minutes taking in the utter failure on my
part and took a few deep breaths.

I pulled away from the neighborhood, deep in
thought, and waiting for the car heater to kick
into gear. I was about 90 minutes from home
with a long stretch on the Mass Pike, a thruway
that cuts through Massachusetts all the way out
of greater Boston to the New York line. A late-
night ride along that thruway presented the
perfect time to reflect. The road was void of the
hustle and bustle of the morning, with only a
few cars and truck making their way into the
darkness. The night was brightened a bit by the
white snowbanks along the way, with a sky that
was clear as could be. The stars off in the

distance seemed comforting to me on the ride home.

I was not a fan of random music on a radio station so my choices to break the silence were sports radio or finding one of my CDs on the backseat floor. Born and raised in Buffalo, sports radio wasn't appealing in Boston, especially after all of the Super Bowl losses. Reaching around the seat to find a CD was a bit risky when traveling at a high speed. So I chose silence as I passed the familiar rest stops that marked the distance from home with the familiar illuminating signs of gas stations, fast food, and parking lot lights filled with truckers.

Stopping at any highway rest stop after 9 p.m. is probably a similar feeling anywhere in the country. Everyone moved a bit slower than you remember from the morning. The french fry aroma hit you as you entered the building and it was a mix of people working late, truckers, and out-of-state travelers. But it was always there, 24/7, and they became my beacons in the night to make my way home.

The funny part about silence, it makes your thoughts stand out, and you can hear them dancing around in your head. Tonight was no different. Was this just a bunch of unreasonable people who wanted to torment me and see me shaken? I mean, we are one store in a neighborhood with countless other stores. Why single us out? A few minutes of pity was the warm-up to getting to a better place.

The next 30 minutes on my ride home was spent breaking down what I didn't do that I should have. I never spoke to the supervisor to get their insights of any ongoing issues in the community. I was not in tune with our active community channels of communication. I knew everything about the details of the store—the store management and financials—but I didn't have a proactive outreach in place for the neighborhood we were serving. I wasn't making a substantial effort to ask the community, "How can we be a better neighbor?" I may not have lived there, but we operated our business there, and that should be considered a responsibility to connect. I mentally accepted the responsibility and moved past the pity portion of the night.

The next 30 minutes was spent thinking about how this may be a problem with other communities and could be widespread. At least I'm hearing it from this group. The thought of other neighborhoods having concerns, and I'm not hearing from them, caused me real concern. We need to not only solve this problem, but we need to have an outreach program where we could be part of the solution.

I reflected on the faces of the people in the meeting I just left. They represented a seriousness and passion to make their communities safe, vibrant, and a place they are proud to call home. I could see in their eyes that they were looking to me for solutions, cooperation, and to hear their voices. It wasn't a personal vendetta against me. I was the neighbor who should have listened more closely. And tonight, I heard them, loud and clear. We needed to become familiar faces, rather than people who show up once in a blue moon. We would be present and hear all the issues we were facing and take actionable steps to fix them. That night was a gift, not a failure. I started to feel a sense of gratitude for their brutal honesty.

The final 30 minutes were spent planning how I would resolve the issues I heard that night. I needed to find out when the next meeting was, get with the supervisor, and hash out every individual issue we were facing. I wanted to hear it all—the good, the bad and the ugly. No holding back, even if we fell down on the job somewhere, which, it was clear, we did. I wanted to have all of the details.

We requested to be on the next neighborhood meeting agenda and this time I was ready. One of the most outspoken people at the last meeting whispered to me on my way up to speak, "I'm surprised you're back."

I wasn't quite sure if that was a jab or a compliment. But honestly, I took it as a bit of inspiration. I'm glad too, I thought.

I addressed four distinct areas:

- Here's what we did wrong and admitted my mistakes (I accept responsibility—we can do better).
- Here's what we plan to do in correcting those issues (I respect you and want to do better).
- Here is my commitment to you in the future (I want to stand by you and stay connected).
- Tell me if I've heard you fully and addressed your concerns. (Confirm I heard you and didn't miss anything important to you).

We introduced the supervisor for that area and committed to attending all future meetings. We had a back-and-forth discussion that I really enjoyed. I noticed how powerful words can be when you truly listen without thinking about what's coming next. Listening is something I improved on over time. That's most likely what Sister Mary Michaels meant in the fifth grade when she said, "Mr. Hart, I want your undivided attention." Without listening, you really can't make progress or establish long, meaningful relationships.

There were still some tough criticisms, but they were now conversations instead of me trying to deflect. We received some light applause at the end, and I was now seeing smiles around the room. Even my biggest critic gave me a quick smile on the way back to my seat. Not an "I'm your friend now" smile, but a smile, nonetheless. That alone felt like a weight was lifted from my shoulders. I felt elated really. We stayed at the meeting from beginning to end. We wanted to hear all the concerns and happenings within the neighborhood. We were, after all, part of the neighborhood.

In future meetings, we sometimes brought food. Not as a bribe, but rather the type of gesture you would make when attending a neighborhood cookout. Maybe it harkens back to memories of my mother always insisting you never visited someone empty handed. For her, it was typically a coffee cake when we visited with her friends for midday tea or potato salad for the summer family cookout. For us, it was typically potato chips, candy, and some beverages. Quite honestly, I started to know many of those local residents better than my neighbors at home. That may not be saying much since I'm more of a "head nod" neighbor without much verbal interaction. But I enjoyed getting to know them.

The cold room, filled with weary but determined neighbors, was a little warmer now. It wasn't perfect, but perfection wasn't the goal. Being a good neighbor who cared was all they were asking for.

My Moment of Reflection

I learned a number of lessons that night that I will carry throughout my life. It was an experience that, at the time, seemed like an utter failure, (note—it was). But it provided me with a blueprint on how to avoid future disasters. It was a gift that I open again and again.

First, I needed to be completely honest with myself. I wasn't prepared for this meeting. I thought showing up was all I needed to do. That was my first mistake. The people attending the meeting were taking time out of their day to make their neighborhood a better place. I needed to match their determination with preparation.

Next, I needed to understand that what was transpiring outside the four walls of the store was just as important as what was happening inside. How we cooperate and harmonize with the community can directly impact our success. If that was true in this case, it was true in every neighborhood we operated in. We broadened the outreach to other communities and made sure we participated even when we were not on the agenda. Community outreach was a responsibility.

The third lesson I learned is the importance of team participation in community activities. We needed the store teams to understand that we support the community and want to do our part in enhancing the environment we control. Most employees live in the communities they work in, so we needed their efforts and ideas to make this part of our culture.

Everyone makes mistakes throughout their life. Dwelling on your mistake and beating yourself up is one way, and understandable—but only for a short time.

Meeting your failures head-on, and finding your inner grit takes a conscious determination to not let a situation break you. Don't shy away from mistakes—learn from them and admit them out loud. Leaders who admit mistakes to their teams open the door to transparency. And in these moments, we become inspired and inspire those around us.

Chapter 7

A Boss, A Mentor, and a Friend

"Our chief want in life is somebody who will make us do what we can."

—Ralph Waldo Emerson

I t was a particularly hot and muggy July day as I made my way into the office, turned off the alarm, and went up the stairs and into the paneled hallway of offices. I was new in my current role as Chief Operating Officer, learning to navigate when to get into the details, and when to let others take the lead. I had been reporting to the CEO Bob Gordon for quite some time now. But this role was different. Bob was expecting me to be more strategic than tactical, which I was excited about. At the same time, I felt a bit unsure of how I would measure up to these new responsibilities.

When I first started reporting to Bob, it was nerve-wracking to say the least. Bob was a Harvard grad. I checked the "some college" box. Bob spent his time away from work bettering the lives of people in Dnepropetrovsk through humanitarian efforts. I recycled on Saturdays and got to know the semi-retired guy at the tiny corner shop I would stop at for coffee and bagels after my good deeds of separating paper and plastic were accomplished. Bob had flown all over the world. I flew to Las Vegas for a trade show. Bob lived in a high rise in Boston. I lived in the woods way down the Mass Pike.

Bob also had a vocabulary that would sometimes call for some research. Before Google was at my fingertips serving up definitions, synonyms, and the origin of the word, I depended on the paperback Merriam-Webster's dictionary I kept in the right-hand top drawer of my metal desk. As Bob's emails came through, I would slide open that drawer and flip through muttering something like, "Egregious – hmm. E-g-r-e-g...oh, that means really bad."

We had different backgrounds, to say the least. But we always seemed to work well together, and he never made me feel less worldly than him. We have all met the kind of people that make you feel inferior because of their status in society. Bob was not that person.

The first time I met Bob, I was running the register as a store manager. It was late at night, and he was with some friends, most likely just leaving dinner. I never met Bob before, so I had no idea what he looked like. He approached the register and said, "Are you the new manager?" "Yes," I replied, "have we met?" "I'm Bob Gordon, I work in the office." He didn't announce himself as the CEO, or owner, or with a "do you know who I am" persona. Simply, "I work in the office." But I immediately knew he was the owner since that was the name stamped on my weekly paycheck.

I was working a double shift for the third night in a row, exhausted. I'm pretty positive I seemed like a low energy individual that did not make a good impression in our first 30-second exchange. In those moments, you don't have time to say,

"Sorry, I'm usually much more energetic than this but I haven't had a day off in a while and we are down three full-time people." I would have sounded a bit unhinged, so I just left it with "Nice to meet you." I never dreamt that I would eventually be working side by side with Bob for years to come.

Bob knew about my background, yet gave me the confidence to serve as his Chief Operating Officer. It's not a position I was planning to ever hold. In fact, I never really had a career plan, or these dreams of "moving up the corporate ladder." I always focused on the responsibilities in front of me. That was the plan. That was it. I think a big part of that approach was the inspiration that always came from my love of working with my team on new initiatives or projects. We would approach every challenge with an energy and passion that drove our success. I didn't need to look into the future for my career goal—I was living it each day and that was good enough for me.

On Friday afternoons I would venture down to Bob's office, walking along the paneled hallway, for my weekly meeting. Doris Gordon, Bob's wife, had an office right across from his and I would always poke my head around the corner to say hello before my meetings and she would always give me a warm smile. On a Friday afternoon, I always looked forward to that moment.

Doris was someone I could always count on for words of wisdom I needed at the right time. She once told me, "Bob likes you because you tell him what others are afraid to say to him. You're brutally honest. That's good, keep it up."

I wasn't always the person in the room who was brave enough to have those difficult conversations, certainly not as I was growing up. I can't actually pinpoint when it changed, but I'd imagine it came from years of managing a store that never closed. You would get turned upside down quickly if you didn't deal with your daily hurdles honestly, quickly, and effectively. Holding back wasn't an option.

Difficult conversations need certain ingredients to be productive. I would have my facts in order, be specific about the issue, and why I thought this discussion was important. There were times when Bob would bring this up in our weekly larger meetings with others and say something like, "Tom said I needed to…[fill in the blank with whatever we discussed last week]." Everyone would look down the table at me. I would be thinking, *"You weren't supposed to say that part out loud*. But that's what I loved about Bob. He was transparent, and honest, always. I never doubted for a split second that Bob wouldn't be straight with me.

Doris was Director of Foodservice and Special Projects, and she was the kinder, gentler other half of my boss that not everyone is lucky enough to get to know and confide in. Besides her advice, we could also share a laugh about our love of "Seinfeld" or the next great deli item we would introduce. She also brought a very pragmatic view to our discussions. "Just go ahead and do it," she'd say, with a wave of her hand, adding "stop talking about it already." We would all look at each other like, "She's right, enough talking." I'm sure she saved us countless hours of unnecessary chatter with this simple approach. The Doris approach of "enough already" is something I would embrace in many future endeavors.

During my Friday hourly meetings with Bob, we would cover a lot of ground. The first time I stepped into Bob's office with just the two of us, my mind was racing. We were always in a group meeting prior to this, and now it was just us. When I closed the door, the entire outside world seemed to disappear, and the quietness made me feel like I was on full display. I had my yellow pad, a pen, some paperwork to reference, and a boatload of anticipation.

I learned quickly to prepare for any question Bob may have. At the time I was managing operations, marketing, human resources, and properties. We would cover it all. I would watch him click through saved emails in a folder with my name on it.   I remember thinking, "how many emails are in that folder." At times it seemed like a bottomless pit of email subjects. Then we would move on to financials or Bob's visit to the stores. Digital personal cameras were just breaking into the mainstream, replacing film, and Bob of course was the first to pick one up. Sometimes from across the desk we would scroll through photos he had taken during his visits. It was a slideshow of the good, the bad, and the ugly. *I need one of these cameras*, I thought. As our relationship grew stronger, I would start adding my own agenda items to our meeting. I would seek his advice in certain situations, and he would lean back a bit in his chair to listen or lean forward to ask a few questions.

Bob also had a way of surprising you and pushing you completely out of your comfort zone. He didn't nudge, it was a giant push. I always knew when Bob entered the hallway in the morning as the familiar sound of the wheels of his laptop computer bag rolled along the carpeted hallways right past my office. One day, he very casually asked me to fill in for him that night for a local dinner invite he received and couldn't attend. *Sure*, I thought, thinking it would be some city event at a local hotel. It was not. It was a dinner party held at the home of Professor Gates, a Harvard professor. *You have to be kidding me*, I thought. *How can I carry a conversation at a dinner party with a Harvard professor?* I knew this wasn't a request with "no" as an option, so I said, "Certainly," to Bob and walked back to my office and closed the door. Barbara is coming with me, I thought. My wife always shored up my lack of confidence with a "you got this" look. This would be needed tonight.

We parked the car as close to the professor's house as possible and walked down the street. It was still really hot and muggy, and a suit and tie made me feel like it was 150 degrees out. As we made our way down the street, I fussed with my top button under my tie. My shirt size had not kept pace with my late-night eating, so the button decided to pop off as I was fixing it. I could see it skip across the sidewalk in slow motion just as we arrived at the professor's front doorstep. I looked at my wife Barbara with a, "This will be funny one day, but not right now expression." But she laughed, pushed my tie up and said, "No one will even notice." And she gave me that "you got this" look that snapped me back into the moment. She delivered, as expected. I shrugged it off as we made our way up the walkway.

We stepped onto the porch and knocked on the front door and there was no turning back. The home was filled with people. In every room, there were the typical small circles of conversations and soft, friendly chatter. The walls were adorned with art from all over the world. The professor quickly greeted us and could not have been nicer. He thanked us for coming and introduced his wife and a few other people. We felt very comfortable and were quickly put at ease.

I feared we would have to talk about the latest country we visited ("Canada," I was prepared to say. "It's lovely."), Act 3 of King Lear, or the details of quantum physics. Or I'd get the dreaded question that I always worried I'd be asked: "Where did you go to college?" None of these nightmare scenarios happened. We had terrific conversations and enjoyed some appetizers. I honestly couldn't identify what I was eating, but it was delicious. My experience with appetizers up to this point were pizza rolls, mozzarella sticks, and potato skins, so this was rather enjoyable.

The dinner party was held to celebrate the launch of a play about a runaway slave, Moses, and took place in the 1800s. We were able to watch a segment of the upcoming performance in the living room. The guests went completely silent, and we could only hear a clock ticking in the background. Everyone stood completely still. We were a few feet away as the performers sang and delivered a powerful, memorable experience that I will forever cherish. Barbara and I looked at each other like it was a moment we would never forget. The voices felt like they wrapped around us as they carried through the room. Such talent. Such beauty. As they finished their performance, the guests lingered for a bit. But it was soon time to get on the road for that long trek home. Home was more than an hour west of Harvard and it had been a long day.

I loosened my tie once again to breathe comfortably as we made our way back to the car. I remember thinking how lucky I was to have Bob pushing me out of my comfort zone and sending me to an experience I would treasure for so many years. When I got back to my office, I remember describing the event to Bob and he could tell it was a powerful experience for me, most likely from the excitement in my voice.

We decided to ask the director of the play if the cast would come to sing at the conclusion of our upcoming managers' meeting. To our delight, he accepted, and their powerful, uplifting performance had the entire company on their feet, singing and having a great time. Today, if I close my eyes, I still vividly remember the final song, "This little light of mine." I can see the managers' smiling faces and the stress rolling off their shoulders. I thanked the performers for this unbelievable experience and said to them, "They wanted more and were calling for an encore. It was incredible." He said with a smile, "That's how you want to leave the performance, with the audience on their feet and wanting more." Amen to that.

Bob gave me many more opportunities over our years working together and even hired a coach for my personal development. Bob expected a lot but gave back so much more.

These days, sitting on our back patio in the quiet of the morning, in a state of reflection, I often find myself drifting back on our history together. The simplest of things come to mind. A dinner we shared together in Boston. A difficult moment that we resolved together. Those private conversations on a Friday afternoon and giving me the opportunity of a lifetime—being part of a team that accomplished so much.

I have a profound sense of gratitude for having Bob in my life. John unlocked my grit, my father was my role model, and Bob built my confidence and strengthened my determination in life. Recently, I was fortunate to be invited to attend Bob's 80th birthday celebration and thank him. I enjoyed seeing him smile as he was surrounded by family and friends who were so glad to be part of Bob's life. For that moment, I am truly thankful.

You see, Bob started out as my boss, but became my mentor and is now my friend.

My Moment of Reflection

I was fortunate to be surrounded by people with grit and determination my entire life. My career was full of long days, sometimes late nights, and always challenging with a daily gut-check to keep pushing forward. I always felt we shared an unspoken bond in many ways. But even people with incredible grit benefit from having a mentor. Grit without mentorship can go off track, leaving you rudderless as you march through life. There's a compelling reward in mentorship that comes from purely making a difference.

There's a story that has been reshaped, repackaged, and told in various versions, originally by Loren Eiseley, but I like the main point. It's a story about a man walking along the beach just before dawn. Off in the distance, he sees a young girl moving about, picking something up off the sand and throwing it, gently and with great care, into the ocean. As he comes closer to the young girl, he notices thousands of starfish washed onto the shore. As he approached her, he said, "Young girl, what are you doing?" She replied, "The sun will be up soon and if I don't throw them into the ocean, they will die." The man looked at her with disbelief, "There are thousands of starfish all over the beach. The sun will be up shortly, you can't possibly make a difference." She picked up a starfish, looked at it, and gently tossed it back into the ocean. She then looked up at the man and said, "I made a difference to that one."

I love this story for its simplicity. Yes, it's true, we can't mentor every person we encounter. But it is important to be mindful of how your interactions can impact others.

Bob made a difference in my life. John made a difference in my life. My father made a difference in my life. My wife made a difference in my life. So many people you meet become a part of who you are through your life in moments. I believe and have tried to model the importance of mentorship throughout my career. I'm hopeful I made a difference along the way by giving back to others.

We can get busy and move on to the next project without giving much thought to the people around us. How can you make a difference? Perhaps it may mean you take time out of the overbooked schedule to see how people are doing. It may mean taking the last five minutes of a meeting to ask how they're doing. Reflect back in life to when you needed that inspiration the most and were fortunate enough to have someone there for you. I now consider it an obligation to give back to others, but also consider it a gift that you can give over and over again.

We can make a difference. Be present. With one person, one moment at a time.

Chapter 8

A Cold Chicago Morning, A Warm Moment To Cherish

"You must collect moments. Those will be the true wealth of your soul."

—R Liviu C. Tudose

I was walking the streets of Chicago, headed to the convention center in the early morning hours of October 2017 as my mind was taking a stroll down memory lane. It had been 10 years since I struck out on my own to start my own consulting company, leaving my life in retail behind. It was not an easy decision, certainly not one that came without reservation. I was working with a great group of people and life was good. But something was missing. I wanted to see what kind of future I could build with a business supporting the very people I worked side by side with my entire life. I had a burning desire to give it a shot and it kept growing stronger with each passing day.

In July of 2007, as Barbara and I were enjoying a glass of wine at Bertucci's I looked at her and said, "It's time." I had been talking about it for several months, but I was now absolutely sure in my heart. She looked at me and said "I'm with you. Go for it. Tomorrow."

Now here I was in Chicago to once again showcase Dashboard Advantage—a Software-as-a-Service company that helped organizations improve store execution. I created it with my partner, Sam Coons, as an offshoot to my consulting business, but soon became a full-fledged company. Most teams at the time were still documenting issues related to stock shortages, repair needs, and store conditions on paper, we could offer a better way to capture this information through our app and online platform.

I never planned to co-found a tech company. I

certainly wasn't a tech genius. I wasn't even entirely clear on the difference between upload and download. But I always had the latest gadget – having relished in purchasing my first tablet – a Blackberry PlayBook. I still remember the day when I arrived at a trade show with my PlayBook and bedazzled the crowd as they all wanted to see this new device. Shortly thereafter, other devices like the iPad soon turned my PlayBook into a large coaster for my cup of coffee. Being first isn't always a pathway to success. Nonetheless, I was a fan of using technology throughout my life, so it seemed like a good path to the future.

The walk to the convention center had all the trappings of a beautiful autumn morning; wet leaves gathered about the walkways, trees half bare and preparing for the first snow, jackets and sweaters were making their appearance after a summer of hibernation, and people scampered off to meet the day kissed by a cool breeze. It seemed to be the perfect wake-up call. I'd tossed and turned the night before with the usual trade show jitters. The early walk was the perfect remedy to shake off a restless night's sleep. I was confident that the support requests coming in wouldn't skip a beat. I had the privilege of having my son Nathan coordinating the efforts of the customer requests and was great at getting things done. He had been working with me for almost 10 years at this point.

As I reached the exhibition hall at the McCormick Center, I could feel the energy coming alive that would soon greet over 24,000 convenience store operators roaming about in search of new ideas and perhaps some needed reassurance that they were on the right track.

I always marveled at the early-morning hour of a convention coming alive. Volunteers would be finding the way to their stations. The hallways were sometimes half-lit, forklifts were darting around, and bucket trucks were getting the last of the hanging signs in place. Off in the distance, but always a few minutes away in any direction, I could smell freshly-brewed coffee, then eventually the aroma of roller grill hot dogs, pizza coming out of the ovens, and, of course, fried chicken. The colorful lights bouncing off the booths showcasing frozen drinks, gas pump technology, giant candy displays, and every type of beverage you can imagine had representatives ready to strut their stuff. What you typically found in a small space in a local convenience store was now surrounded by smart designs and smiling booth hosts. It was like everything tasted better in these temporary settings, "Why yes, this is the best fried chicken I've ever had in my life," you'd think to yourself as you finished the two-bite sample on a tiny square napkin. It could also be that you skipped breakfast, stayed up too late, and are working through lunch, but all in all, people love trade show samples.

I was entering the hall alone that morning, probably because I was arriving five hours before the first attendee would grace the entrance of the hall. I always wanted to venture out early at trade shows or any event. Perhaps it is a continuation of my father's influence of us entering the side door of Trico Plant #1 well before most people were probably awake for the workday.

I finally arrived at booth 3162, which is where I would call home for the next three days. No fried chicken samples or brick-oven pizzas here. But we did have mints in a bowl that seemed quite popular. Being alone in my thoughts on the trade show floor, admiring the backdrop of our booth design, computers glowing, handouts stacked, and business cards in place – I stood back and took in the moment. I knew the mental and physical toll it took to get to this point. It was not a small price to pay, that's for sure. But these early moments of reflection were priceless—and I realized this is why I enjoy the quietness of the morning. If I jumped in minutes before the crowd, this moment of reflection and appreciation would be washed away quickly.

I popped in one of those delicious mints, sat on our trade show stool we'd had for the last 10 shows and let my mind drift back to our first trade show— it was not a bastion of confidence building moments.

I remember saying hello as I passed by the president of a rather large company during a nighttime pre-show event. He said hello back, stopped, and asked me "What is Dashboard Advantage?" I was expecting him to nod and keep walking. I was not ready for this impromptu engagement outside of my 10 by 10 booth. I stammered and said something like, "We have a solution you use for, well we capture, well we help teams... Here's my card." The look on his face was one that screamed, "No idea what you just said." But he was quite kind and said, "Have a good show," and caught up to some folks on the other side of the room. In my mind, I was Homer Simpson in a "Doh!" head-slapping moment. I was not a seasoned salesperson to say the least.

Early on I couldn't get my 30-second pitch down to get anyone to stay put for a demonstration of our solution. People hurried down the aisles at the speed of the rabbit in Alice in Wonderland. I would stand at the edge of the carpeted booth and get out a few words like "Do you have a minute", which would immediately be met with either a hurried rejection, "No thanks", or they would just turn their head in the opposite direction pretending they had no idea we just had eye contact.

The entire three days was like emotional pinball. One moment, people would love what you have to offer—"That's pretty slick, they'd say." Next moment—they look at you like they are sorry they stopped and were looking for the first moment to break away. You could almost sense their energy gently pulling away from you, as you try to find a magic word to break the spell. But each time someone crossed the threshold of our booth space, a new burst of energy would arrive. That was what kept me going: the moment-to-moment opportunity was exhilarating.

Beyond the allure of a trade show scene, I would also meet with people at their offices to give a pitch, hoping for someone to give us a shot. Early on, I remember meeting in the offices of our biggest opportunity yet. We had about 20 people packed in the conference room, ready to hear about our solution. Stacks of paper, laptops, vendor samples of candy, and beef jerky filled the tables as the team prepared themselves for a day of information overload. As the person making a presentation before me wrapped up, I got ready. And I was ready — working late the night before to get my presentation in order, considering every potential ROI question, and how we can help the organization.

About three minutes into my presentation, the Vice President, who was a last-minute invite, stops me and asks: "What is this about?" He had a look on his face that resembled, "Hey pal, I believe you are wasting my time." I gave a quick 30-second summary to which he replied, "That is a really stupid idea. We don't need that. Let's move on. What's next on the agenda?" as he turned his head away from me.

Huh? All eyes were back on me as to my next move. Let's break it down, I was just told: 1. You have a stupid idea. 2. You need to move on. 3. What's next? I looked to find a few friendly faces around the table, but no rescue was in sight. There were just a few shrugged shoulders like "Sorry about that." Pretty sure that was my queue to pack up my things and get out of the building. I brought my own projector, so it took me even longer to depart as the power cords snaked around laptops and under the table. Humiliating.

As I exited the room, I remember thinking, *Did we create a solution no one was asking for and no one wanted? Did we just come up with New Coke?* But we pushed on and slowly we convinced enough people to give us a shot to make us a viable company with a good reputation.

This was not my initial focus as I started off on my own. Early on, my business was based around consulting. The first year I had $1,500 in income and about $35,000 in business expenses. You don't have to be a financial wizard to realize that is not sustainable. The financial crisis in the U.S. was starting to rear its ugly head in my first year, and hiring consultants seemed like a budget line-item people wanted to eliminate. In fact, I found that the word "consultant" was synonymous with "expensive" or "non-essential."

But a glimmer of hope appeared one day. A colleague of mine gave me a lead that provided a surge of confidence—a sure thing. "Call this guy—I told him about you. He will hire you on the spot—just tell him I recommended you."

Well, I called, introduced myself and gave the reason for my call. When I got about 20 seconds into the conversation, he yelled out, "You called at the worst possible time" and hung up. It was a desktop phone with a handset, so it was a really effective, old-fashioned hang-up. At that moment in my basement office, I thought *What am I doing thinking I could become a consultant?* I must have been crazy. But I am here now and need to make this work. My mindset needed to be steeped in finding new ways to make this work. I decided then and there that this was going to work. Re-focus and dig in. Grit and determination, filled with some hope, carried the day.

Well, that same company that hung up on me changed leadership a few months later, and the new VP of Operations called *me*! I almost fell out of my chair. I went out, presented to him (no phone calls this time) and he said—you're hired, for a six-month contract, and we'll take it from there. I worked with them for about seven years after that. We ended up laughing about the episode when their CFO hung up on me. In fact, I even got to talk with the CFO about it. He said he didn't remember, but even if he did, he probably would like to avoid the topic. Life has a funny way of turning one of the lowest points in your life into a memory that seems less harmful in the rearview mirror.

I'm convinced these abrupt dismissals made me more determined than ever to make these ventures successful. No different than sleeping on a porch, working double shifts, or getting blasted by the neighborhood in a community meeting—I've always found a way to internalize these struggles and turn them into energy to find the right path.

Often people would say, "It must be great to own your own business." And that's true! But then often they add, "Must be nice to not have someone breathing down your neck." That's not true! Owning a business for me was often a day filled with wins, losses, moments of great happiness and satisfaction, mixed in with many sleepless nights and moments of self-doubt.

My Moment of Reflection

Starting my own business would not have been possible without all the experiences I've had throughout life. John, my first manager back in Buffalo, taught me about responsibility and instilled a sense of self-discipline at 18-years old. He taught me early on about giving it your all on each and every shift. He noticed the small things in business and showed me how they made a difference. Not everything is a giant win, but rather several small victories woven together in search of excellence.

Bob Gordon gave me the confidence to take the leap. He cast me out of my comfort zone but gave me the support I needed to learn new business skills that would help me build a future on my own. The opportunities I was provided to lead a team, solve complex problems, create, and build brands were the opportunities of a lifetime that helped me in every aspect of my life.

My father taught me about hard work and never giving up. He instilled in me a sense of responsibility to my family, that I was capable and could do anything I set my mind to. He was always my biggest advocate and never doubted me for one second.

And my wife Barbara was always in my corner. Whenever I was feeling down and out, she brought me back and gave me the energy to push forward. I remember early on at our first trade show she could sense my anxiety. She walked over and whispered to me "You got this." That's all I needed to hear. She always had my back, and I always knew I could count on her to be there for me. Beyond any skills I acquired over the years, that was the biggest factor in my success. Being supported by someone so deeply, and that same person is the love of your life. It doesn't get any better than that.

I also learned the value of relationships. Decades of relationship building and creating a wide network of people throughout my life was incredibly helpful. Many I would work with, others I would seek advice from during a time of uncertainty. Some I met along the way for only a few brief moments, but I learned a new perspective from them that I would tuck away. The opportunity to be involved in industry events, or collaborative efforts that expanded my network, gave me a deep sense of connection. I wasn't alone. Those relationships take time and nurturing to be built one by one. I can't put a value on the ability to be able to reach out to someone and ask for 15 minutes of their time to get their advice. Or meeting someone for lunch to run your business plan by them and get their feedback.

Without this network of bright, supportive people, the road would have been rockier and possibly a dead-end. But I did have these connections, and I'm grateful for each one of them.

I'm not through meeting new people, learning from those around me and reaching out to those I've met along the way to share a moment as the journey continues.

Final Chapter

One More Moment

"At the end, one didn't remember life as a whole but as just a string of moments."

—David Levien

There comes a point in your life, or at least in mine, that you become a bit more reflective than your hard-charging younger years. I think I noticed it around 10 years ago when I became choked up at the Subaru commercial with the aging dog riding around with the owner, visiting a farm - and well - I started getting misty eyed. What is happening to me? Doris might say I was verklempt—Yiddish for overcome with emotion. But as time goes on, you get used to it and eventually just go with it.

As I looked back on my experiences, I realized that throughout my lifetime many people came into my world, and in an instant, they were gone. At least it seems that way when I ran across someone from my past and began to count the years since we last spoke. We say the customary goodbyes and say, "Let's keep in touch." But it's hard. Life is busy and complicated and, inevitably, people that were once front-and-center in your life slip away.

As I was writing my story, I didn't know what the ending would look like. But as I continued to share my experiences about the people in my life, I was clearly wishing for one more moment with many of them. I won't get that chance in many cases, as some are no longer with us. But if I could, those moments would go something like this.

Ron, the Royal Cola Driver in Buffalo

I can see the agony in your face and the pain in your hands. You have worked tirelessly in your life, even in your old age. You must have had someone you loved deeply at home to be this devoted to work, as you endured so much pain. I wish I could have met your family to tell them how much I admired you and enjoyed our times together as a young man. I would ask more about you—what makes you happy and how you spend your weekends. I'd cherish one more moment unloading your truck together, hoisting the rickety wooden crates onto your two-wheeler, across the frozen lot that seemed to fight against you with each step, and sending you off with a steaming cup of hot coffee to ward off the Buffalo cold. I would share how I loved hearing "Ron's here" and seeing you pull on the lot as I grabbed my gloves to meet you outside, my heart happy to see you step down from the truck. I would tell you how much I missed you when we parted ways and that you were a role model inspiring me to work hard despite the difficulties handed to you in life.

John my manager
I wish I could see you and your crooked smile come walking through the door at Red Lalley's Grill once again as I waved you over to the seat I saved you at the bar and share one more draft beer together. I would tell you that I cherished every second of our conversations and when

they ended, I immediately looked forward to the next one. I'd want you to know that when I visited Buffalo years after leaving, you were the only person outside my family I would want to see. Not the people I grew up with, but the man who gave me the opportunity of a lifetime and never even realized it. I would tell you how you inspired me to choose my own path in life and instilled confidence in me to find my inner grit that would carry me many times through life. As we both headed for our cars, departing one last time, I would be thankful for having met you as you pulled away, your taillights fading into the night as if to say, "You got this Thomas, my friend."

My Team

If I had one more moment with my team in a conference room, I would load it with fresh hot pizza that often became dinner on late nights and share how you lifted me so much more than I ever lifted you. I would tell you how fortunate I was to know and work with each and every one of you. I would share some laughs and reminisce about our successes as well as our failures, as they both delivered lifelong lessons in our journey together. We would remember our marathon meetings, driving through snowstorms to reach each other, late-night phone calls with every type of emergency you could imagine, moments of doubt, and wins that we never thought were imaginable. I would share my belief that I honestly felt that once we closed the door and got down to business, nothing was impossible if we stuck together. Our kindred spirit we held was special, unspoken, and always alive and well when we entered any room together.

I would also want to hear about your families and your dreams. I would tell you how much I enjoyed it when you'd drop by my office, and we would get lost in conversation until one of us realized it was way past dinner time and we would quickly head out to get started on the pathway home.

I'd also thank you for the opportunity to lead such a talented team of people. It was the honor of a lifetime forever burned into my memory with a fire that is eternal.

Tom at Charlestown

I would say thank you so much for visiting me on the midnight shift when I felt so emotionally empty and physically drained. My spirits boosted immediately as the front door swung open and your big smile yelled out my name in your Boston accent that was as thick as your mustache. I would love to make you another cup of coffee, that fuel you seemed to live on, and just share some more laughs together. I would thank you for holding me steady when my daughter was in a serious car accident in only a way you could do, knocking me back into reality with your tough, townie persona. I would like to hear more about your life, what makes you happy and what's on your mind. You were always thinking of others, working three jobs as you marched through life, and I'm convinced you never took time for yourself. I would take that moment to be present for you and listen to whatever is on your mind. I would thank you for a friendship that will live in me forever, even as we drifted apart.

My Late-Night Friends

To my favorite customer Marjorie who used to arrive around 4 a.m. each morning to wipe down the counters and make coffee. You didn't want a job, but you loved to be there, visit, and help. We had so many laughs and special moments together, even if they were in tiny increments each day. Our friendship was strong with a 40-year age difference that didn't even seem noticeable. If I could have one more moment, I would tell you that when you were busy cleaning and brewing fresh coffee, you left a warm spot on my heart that would stay there forever. The world needs more of your kind of kindness, smiles, and genuine friendship.

To Bo the policeman who often checked up on me, I would say thank you. You steadied my nerves and made me feel safer with your presence, but more importantly your genuine interest in how I was doing meant so much.

To Bobby the *Boston Globe* delivery driver, thank you for your warm and friendly smiles that I looked forward to each night. You could have just tossed the papers in the door and left, but you didn't. You made sure we connected, said hello, and shared a laugh together as we settled our weekly bill.

My Community Leaders
Thank you for allowing me into your community to share your concerns and speak honestly with me. You taught me so much about the importance of being a good neighbor in business and how we impacted your daily life. But you also taught me how to rebound from past mistakes. You were tough on me when I needed you to be, but you didn't hold a grudge. Being in your presence helped me learn how important it is to stay connected in the world around you and the impact we can make by caring, being honest, and working together in a meaningful way.

My father

I wish we could have one more breakfast together at Teddy's on Abbott Road. I would smile when you ordered your predictable breakfast: eggs sunny side up, rye toast, and hash with home fries. I would ask you more about when you and mom were dating. Where did you go and when did you fall in love? I would ask more about your experiences in WWII and what you were feeling during this time. I'd want to know more about your parents and what it was like to grow up in the depression.

I loved hearing the stories you did tell, but only when asked late in life. You were never one to start conversations about yourself. But one story you shared is forever burned in my memory. It was the day you were part of the operation landing on the beaches on D-Day. As the boat made its way across the choppy waters approaching the shore it made a sudden stop and the operator yelled, "Everybody out!" But your Sergeant said, "No way, get us in further — we are too far out." They argued for maybe seconds, finally the boat operator backed up and brought you in considerably closer. If everyone jumped out before the second attempt to get closer to shore, you would have been in too deep of water, too far from shore and most likely drowned carrying the weight of your equipment. So many drowned that day before they reached the shore for this very reason. The way you tell this story so casually always amazed me. I can picture you on the boat, wind and rain whipping against your face, the landing flat bottom boat rocking in the choppy waters and not really sure what to expect when you hit the beach. And you also casually mentioned one of the men dropped the mine detector in the water when they lost their balance. Inspiration, grit, and determination personified.

I would tell you again how sorry I am that you had to bury my brother and no parent should have to bury their children. I know how hard that was for you and how close you both became later in life.

I would tell you that you were the best father a son could ever hope for. You were my hero. You held my rope ladder and supported me without hesitation. I would tell you how much I miss you, if I had one more moment.

But I don't have one more moment Dad. You are still a part of me, of who I am. Nothing can ever take that away. For that, I am forever grateful.

Many More Moments
Most of all, I'd like to honor the person I plan to share many more moments on this journey, my wife Barbara. Thank you for confidence you gave me when I had doubts about my own business during the early rejections day after day. You knew exactly when I needed a push, when I needed to cut myself some slack, when I needed a hug, and even when I needed to change course. I know in my heart I couldn't have made it through any of this without you by my side.

Barbara had a way of knowing when you needed reassurance and love. Not just to me, but also to the people around her. One day early on in our marriage Barbara was shopping at the Christmas Tree Shop. She noticed a centerpiece that would be perfect for the holiday dinner table. She placed it in the cart as she browsed for a few more items to brighten up the home in only a way she could put together. An elderly woman noticed the centerpiece in Barbara's cart, leaned over and softly asked with a smile, "excuse me dear, where did you get that, it's quite beautiful?" Barbara smiled back, pointed to the aisle where she found it and exchanged a pleasant few seconds of conversation you might have with a stranger you meet as you are out and about. Suddenly the woman's husband barked, "We don't need that." Her smile quickly went away, and she seemed to have a cloud of sadness suddenly over her. She quietly thanked Barbara and they each went their separate ways.

It so happened they both approached their cars at the same time. Barbara looked over at the woman as they were loading their goods, took the centerpiece out of her backseat, walked over, and handed it to the woman. "Here I want you to have this, you seemed to like it so much." The woman looked in disbelief at Barbara, obviously touched and thanked her, tears welling up in her eyes. "Are you sure, oh my, that's so kind of you." Barbara snuck a glance over at the irritable husband who seemed to crack a slight smile noting the touching moment.

Now we don't know what happened once they each went their separate ways. But what if that small gesture was the kindness the woman needed so badly at that time? What if it made her husband reflect on how happy the moment of tenderness made his wife feel, and he had been too short lately? Maybe none of this happened. But what if it became a moment she would hold, and cherish from time to time? I'm quite happy thinking about that centerpiece sitting on the dinner table as she shares a holiday meal with her family. Perhaps she sneaks a glance during dinner and smiles to herself about this woman at the Christmas Tree Shop.

These moments, these small gestures, between strangers are what makes life special.

They can come at the perfect point in time.

Barbara was great at making these moments, and still is today.

My Moment of Reflection

I never intended for this story to be about me. It was always about the people around me and how they lifted me through some of my toughest moments. None of my "one more moment" stories are filled with any regret. They are pulling from a lifetime of wonderful memories. They energize me to this very day. I think of it as cherishing the people you meet along the way as you wind your way through life. Remembering how they made you feel, so you can give back along the way.

If I had any dreams for the good that might come from my story it would be for you to recognize the people around you—right now, in this very moment. If you could close your eyes and think of one person you would want to share one more moment—who would it be?

I recently called someone I hadn't spoken to for 18 years. I wanted to tell him how much I appreciated and enjoyed our times together. We shared a few stories and laughed a bit. It didn't have to last long, but I had my one more moment. I plan to make many more in the days ahead.

We run through life focused on what's in front of us to get us through the day, the week, the season. Our life in moments become stitched together and create our history, our legacy. Each day we create the past. But the present is where we can change lives. And it is moment to moment.

Realize now that you are creating memories and may be influencing those around you more than you know. It could be the person you see on the way into work that could use a warm smile. Make their day.

The kids you are sending off to school will be off on their own before you know it. Hug them dearly. They'll cherish it, if not right then and there, they will one day.

A colleague you shared some special moments together, that you haven't spoken to in years. Surprise them with a call.

A parent who took care of you many years ago, but now needs your encouragement, reassurance, and tender moments to cherish when they sit at home, alone, dancing through memories. Pull out a moment, a memory from the past and share why it was special to you. Those moments will warm their hearts.

Embrace mentorship. And most importantly, give back. It's a gift to give over and over. I'm sure John never knew the impact he had on me back in Buffalo at 18 years old, but he changed my life. Think of how you have or could impact someone's life with the simplest of gestures. Don't underestimate small actions. They may come at the exact moment someone needed them.

Time is fleeting and each moment is precious. You may not get a second chance.

Life in moments. Let's create beautiful, life changing moments.

Afterword

"Don't wait for the perfect moment, take the moment and make it perfect."

—Zoey Sayward

T hank you for reading my story. I hope you found the inspiration you needed to make a change you may have been thinking about, mentor someone who needs you, or let someone know how much you appreciate them being in your life.

I would love to hear about your special moments in life and how they impacted you. Send your special moments to: tom@lifeinmoments.com

I'll be sharing these stories on our website www.lifeinmoments.com

I'll also continue to reach out to the people in my life. I hope you'll pick up; I have one more moment to share with you.

Made in the USA
Monee, IL
18 September 2021

77587972R00095